Reactions to Silberman's *Crisis in the Classroom*

With a Response
by Charles E. Silberman

edited by

A. Harry Passow

Teachers College, Columbia University

Charles A. Jones Publishing Company
Worthington, Ohio

Contemporary Educational Issues
National Society for the Study of Education

Farewell to Schools??? Daniel U. Levine and Robert J. Havighurst, Editors

Models for Integrated Education, Daniel U. Levine, Editor

Accountability in Education, Leon M. Lessinger and Ralph W. Tyler, Editors

PYGMALION Reconsidered, Janet D. Elashoff and Richard E. Snow

Reactions to Silberman's CRISIS IN THE CLASSROOM, A. Harry Passow, Editor

1 2 3 4 5 6 7 8 9 10 / 76 75 74 73 72

Library of Congress Catalog Card Number: 78-184314
International Standard Book Number: 0-8396-0018-6

Printed in the United States of America

Series Foreword

Reactions to Silberman's CRISIS IN THE CLASSROOM is one of a group of five publications which constitute the first of a series published under the auspices of the National Society for the Study of Education. Other titles are:

Farewell to Schools??? edited by Daniel U. Levine and Robert J. Havighurst

Accountability in Education, edited by Leon M. Lessinger and Ralph W. Tyler

Pygmalion Reconsidered, by Janet D. Elashoff and Richard E. Snow

Models for Integrated Education, edited by Daniel U. Levine

For more than seventy years the National Society has published a distinguished series of Yearbooks. Under an expanded publication program, beginning with the items referred to above, the Society plans to provide additional services to its members and to the profession generally. The plan is to publish each year a series of volumes in paperback form dealing with current issues of concern to educators. The volumes will undertake to present not only systematic analyses of the issues in question but also varying viewpoints with regard to them. In this manner the National Society expects regularly to supplement its program of Yearbook publication with timely material relating to crucial issues in education.

In this volume Professor Passow has included several original essays prepared by persons with quite varying reactions to the widely read Silberman book. Several previously published reviews of *CRISIS IN THE CLASSROOM* are reprinted. Mr. Silberman has prepared a chapter in which he responds to the comments made by contributors to the volume.

The National Society for the Study of Education wishes to acknowledge its appreciation to all who have had a part in the preparation of this book.

Kenneth J. Rehage
for the Committee on the Expanded Publication
Program of the National Society for the Study of Education

Contributors

Terry Borton, acting director, Affective Education Development Program, Philadelphia Public Schools

David A. Goslin, research sociologist, Russell Sage Foundation

James D. Koerner, program officer, Alfred P. Sloan Foundation

William C. Kvaraceus, chairman, Department of Education, Clark University

Stuart Maclure, editor, *The Times Educational Supplement*, London, England

John S. Mann, assistant professor, Department of Education, University of New Mexico

A. Harry Passow, professor of education, chairman, Department of Curriculum and Teaching, Teachers College, Columbia University

Mark R. Shedd, superintendent of schools, Philadelphia Public Schools

Charles E. Silberman, The Field Foundation

Preface

Reactions to Silberman's CRISIS IN THE CLASSROOM contains a number of carefully written analyses for use in conference, foundations of education classroom, and coffee klatsch discussions of Charles E. Silberman's book. Educators and laymen have been greatly stimulated by this work exploring the ways in which schools, colleges, and mass media educate.

Reactors have written lively essays dealing with one or more of the three parts of *CRISIS IN THE CLASSROOM*. The commentaries present varied and equally balanced attitudes toward the Silberman book. The breadth of this collection of reactions is strengthened by inclusion of several published book reviews on the subject and Charles Silberman's own response completes the volume.

Contents

Chapter

I

Introduction

A. Harry Passow

In this bold new book, the result of a three-and-a-half year study commissioned by the Carnegie Corporation of New York, Charles E. Silberman examines the problems that beset American education with the same intelligence, compassion, and uncompromising honesty that marked his award-winning best seller *Crisis in Black and White.*

With the above sentence, the dust jacket introduces the reader to Silberman's analysis of how and why most schools in America are failing and to his recommendations of what is needed to provide the necessary overhaul from pre-school through graduate education. Not since James B. Conant's Carnegie-supported study, *The American High School Today* (1959), has a book received the kind of attention from professional and lay persons alike that Silberman's *Crisis in the Classroom* is receiving.

Crisis in the Classroom is billed as a study. It is a kind of *study,* an eyewitness report by a perceptive and eloquent journalist who worked with the counsel of an advisory commission of distinguished scholars and educators "with powers of advice but not consent"; traveled here and in England; visited schools, observed classes, interviewed students, teachers, administrators, and citizens interested in schools and schooling; read professional and lay literature critiquing education and proposing changes; and then put it all together to provide an understandable picture of "what is wrong and what needs to be done."

Unlike the Conant Report which was directed initially at boards of education as the influential policy-makers, Silberman aims his book at the widest possible audience—"teachers and students, school board members and tax-payers, public officials and civic leaders, newspaper and magazine editors, television directors, parents and children."(p. vii)*

Silberman's is not an empirical study nor a survey of schools. His data are his own impressions and those of his Carnegie Study staff of three research associates and an administrative assistant. Their reported observations are bulwarked by summaries of pertinent scholarly and journalistic literature. Throughout the book, anecdotal material and quotations are liberally interspersed as ITEMs. The general approach to organizing and conducting the study was not unlike that used by Conant in the three other Carnegie-supported studies—the comprehensive high school, the junior high school, and teacher education.

Originally, the Silberman study was conceived as one of teacher education and, in fact, was titled "The Carnegie Study of the Education of Educators." Silberman soon decided that such a focus was far too restrictive: "One cannot reform teacher education without having some clear notion of what the schools themselves are going to be like—and what they *should* be like."(p. 4) It is the *should* that concerns Silberman a good deal and, as he sees it, *Crisis in the Classroom* became a book on educational purpose, a discussion of "the ways in which schools, colleges, and mass media educate: not only *what* they teach, but *how* they teach, and in particular the manifold and frequently unconscious ways in which how they teach determines what it is that people actually learn."(p. 9)

An individual who sets out to study the whole of American education and, to a limited extent, the society and culture which affect and are affected by it, undertakes no small assignment.† Like all such studies, this one has to be judged on two basic criteria: Are Silberman's analyses of *what is* accurate and complete? Are his proposals for reform valid and comprehensive? Put another way, has Silberman been able to document his conclusions about the condition of education in America and persuade his readers that most public schools, whether slum or suburban, are failing to contribute to the creation and maintenance of a humane society? Have the widely-heralded post-World War II efforts to reform education in America proven as ineffective as he declares? Although Silberman's analyses and arguments are generally quite persuasive, his recommendations for change are less convincing.

---

*Page numbers in parentheses refer to Charles E. Silberman, *Crisis in the Classroom* (New York: Random House, 1970). Copyright 1970 by Charles E. Silberman.

†I can empathize, having undertaken two similar ventures: the first a solo study of education in England *(Secondary Education for All: the English Approach)* and the second, a comprehensive survey involving a staff of 200 *(Toward Creating a Model Urban School System: A Study of the Washington, D. C. Schools).*

Early in his opening chapter, Silberman expresses his indignation at the failures of the schools, using language which has since been widely quoted in the press and other media:

It is not possible to spend any prolonged period visiting public school classrooms without being appalled by the mutilation visible everywhere—mutilation of spontaneity, of joy in learning, of pleasure in creating, of sense of self. . . . Because adults take the schools so much for granted, they fail to appreciate what grim, joyless places most American schools are, how oppressive and petty are the rules by which they are governed, how intellectually sterile and esthetically barren the atmosphere, what an appalling lack of civility obtains on the part of teachers and principals, what contempt they unconsciously display for children as children.(p. 10)

Further, Silberman attributes this situation "not to venality or indifference or stupidity, but to mindlessness,"(p. 10) and by mindlessness, he means "the failure or refusal to think seriously about educational purpose, the reluctance to question established practice."(p. 11) Educators and the general public as well must be involved in a continuous reflection on purpose—on what they are doing and why they are doing it and with serious thought about "the ways in which techniques, content, and organization fulfill or alter purpose."(p. 11)

Silberman's answer to the question, "American Education: Success or Failure?" is that it is *both*—although his analysis must leave the reader with more of a sense of failure and crisis which he views as part of the central paradox of American life: "In almost every area, improvements beyond what anyone thought possible fifty or twenty-five or even ten years ago have produced anger and anxiety rather than satisfaction."(p. 19) His discussion draws heavily on the social critics of our times, looking at many aspects of society, and maintaining that almost all of the professions have an educating role to play which they have either failed to discern or fulfill.

Examination of Problems

Part II is devoted to an examination of "What's Wrong with the Schools." Here Silberman points particularly to the failure of the public school to contribute to "facilitating the movement of the poor and disadvantaged into the mainstream of American economic and social life."(p. 53) He sees us as having exaggerated the *commonness* of the common school and romanticized the schools' contribution to stimulating social and economic ability of the lower classes, whether native-born or immigrant. Whatever measures are used and whatever improvements may have occurred since World War II, the poor and disadvantaged and especially those from racial and ethnic minorities have not achieved *equality* in the schools or in the larger society. Silberman discusses the issues involved in the question whether schools can "make educational outcomes less dependent—substantially less dependent—on social class, ethnicity, and race than they now are?"(p. 69) He draws heavily on the Coleman Report (*Equality of Educational Opportunity*)(1) which related socioeconomic background more closely to achievement than school factors and on the Jensen article, "How Much Can We Boost IQ and Scholastic Achievement?" (*Harvard Educational Review*)(2) which argued that genetic rather than environmental factors accounted for the lower IQ scores and scholastic attainment of blacks. Silberman's ITEMs and examples of schools which he views as *succeeding* with the poor and minorities indicate that he sides with those who believe that what is needed is a genuine conviction that such children can learn and a serious effort to create "an accepting, sympathetic environment" in which they will learn.

However much public schools have failed in the urban slums, there are other defects and failures in schools everywhere which are equally serious. "Education should prepare people not just to earn a living but to live a life—a creative, humane, and sensitive life,"(p. 114) Silberman insists, and "schools must provide a liberal, humanizing education." Certainly schools must provide basic skills of literacy and computation but they must also nurture the capacity to educate oneself. Instead, schools educate for docility, are repressive and stultifying, and are preoccupied with order and control. In order to survive in schools, students and teachers must develop a repertoire of strategies and attitudes. This is inevitable, he believes,

given the obsession with routine and given also the frequency with which students are evaluated, the arbitrariness and mysteriousness (at least to the students) of the criteria by which they are judged, and the importance attached to these evaluations by parents, teachers, colleges, graduate and professional schools, and prospective employers.(p. 146)

Nor have the massive reform efforts of the 1950's and 1960's had an impact on the schools: "the reform movement has produced innumerable changes, and yet the schools themselves are largely unchanged."(p. 159) The reforms dealt with both curriculum and with organization; innovations were widely adopted although it appears that persons in charge of curriculum development were "more alert to the rhetoric of innovation than to the innovations themselves."(p. 172) Silberman's explanation of the failure to bring about substantive reform is that the reformers ignored the experiences of the past reform movements and either ignored or did not understand the "harsh realities of classroom and school organization"(p. 180) which affect the ways teachers teach and schools operate. The most serious error, however, was the failure of modern reformers to consider the questions of educational purpose: "What kind of human beings and what kind of society do we want to produce?" Moreover, modern reformers never considered the curriculum as a whole but attacked the teaching of specific subjects instead with the consequence that critical curriculum areas were almost untouched—the arts and esthetic areas. The "extravagant predictions of wonders to come" from developments in educational technology have hardly been realized. The weakness of computer-assisted instruction is "its insistence that the goals of education not only can, but should, be defined in precise behavioral terms."(p. 201) This, Silberman believes "is a prescription for training and not for education;" it is the latter society needs.

In his analysis of what is wrong with the schools, Silberman ranges far and wide and yet always keeps at least one foot in that institution called the public school. He concludes the section on the failures of educational reform with the observation: "Our most pressing educational problem, in short, is not how to increase the efficiency of the schools; it is how to create and maintain a humane society. A society whose schools are inhumane is not likely to be humane itself."(p. 203) On the other hand, the reverse is equally true in all probability and, in light of his earlier discussion of educating roles of various professions, the interaction of school and society might have received more attention.

Discussion of Change

In Part III, Silberman discusses "How the Schools Should Be Changed." "Schools," he maintains, "can be humane and still educate well. They can be genuinely concerned with gaiety and joy and individual growth and fulfillment without sacrificing concern for intellectual discipline and development." Schools need not be child-centered *or* subject- or knowledge-centered nor need they provide an esthetic and moral education at the expense of the three R's if "their structure, content, and objectives are transformed." (p. 208)

Silberman is much taken with and devotes a lengthy chapter to the so-called *informal education* found in many British primary schools. He describes such programs as "less an approach or method than a set of shared attitudes and convictions about the nature of childhood, learning, and schooling."(p. 208) He sees English informal education as differing from the child-centered programs of the progressive education era and the kind of education advocated by what he calls the *romantic critics* of today (e.g., John Holt, George Dennison, and Paul Goodman). The key difference is in the insistence on the teacher's central role in the educative process: "the responsibility of the teacher means educating them: transmitting, creating, and evoking the skills, values, attitudes, and knowledge that will help them grow into mature, creative, and happy adults."(p. 210)

The informal program has evolved over a period of years, beginning first in the infant schools (ages five to seven) and moving to the junior school (ages seven to eleven), growing out of the pragmatic response of teachers who, Silberman reports, later discovered that there was in fact a considerable body of theory about child growth and development, the learning process, the nature of knowledge, and the aims of education with which to undergird practices they had designed intuitively. These theoretical bases are sketched out by Silberman, and the schools themselves described in some detail—the interest areas, the rich variety of materials, the sound and movement, the pupil engagements, and the teacher as a director and manager of the enterprise. Of significance, Silberman notes, is "the view of childhood as something precious in its own right and not merely a preparation for later life: there is a quality of caring, a concern for children qua children, that tends to be missing in American schools."(p. 230) (Some readers will wonder when this view disappeared from American schools where teachers were criticized precisely for holding it.) The teacher's task is to help the child make a transition from random play activity to more structured purposeful activity to mastery through application. Silberman gives particular attention to something which he claims has no counterpart in American schools—the recognition of expressive movement in primary education, the linking of movement with other areas of learning and experience.

Of course, hard data that might point to the statistical superiority of the informal approach to other approaches are not available. Silberman approves of the suggestion of the National Foundation for Educational Research that "the consequences of different modes of schooling should be sought less in academic attainment than in their impact on how children feel about themselves, about school, and about learning."(p. 262) American advocates of such affective assessments are not unknown but inevitably the data sought to support or reject programs designed to nurture "spontaneity, curiosity, and love of learning" seem to end up dealing with the question of whether or not the children read and compute any better!

Informal education can work as well in the United States as in England, Silberman maintains, and devotes a chapter to bulwark his assertion. He points to ghetto schools in Harlem, rural schools in North Dakota, and other schools across the country where either conscious adaptations or indigenous developments have been initiated and all seem to be working well. Super teachers and super administrators are not required for informal education. Silberman indicates that *experiments* in informal education can be found in various parts of the United States, in real, rather than hothouse situations, involving poor and minority group pupils as well as rural and middle class children. Informal education is not, however, a plan nor a model which can be transplanted from Leicestershire to Louisiana intact. In fact, judging from some of Silberman's examples of informal education in American schools, one suspects that a good many educators are already telling their publics: "Oh sure, we have been doing *it* for quite awhile!" But informality alone is not enough and a balance between two sets of educational objectives—"those concerned with individual growth and fulfillment, and those concerned with the transmission of specific skills, intellectual disciplines, and bodies of knowledge"—is not easy to attain.(p. 322)

If the development of informal education at the elementary level seems to Silberman to be the way to provide education which nurtures intellectual discipline in a free and humane manner, similar reforms at the high school level appear equally desirable and possible. The views of such critics as Arthur Bestor, Edgar Friedenberg, and Paul Goodman (individuals whose criticisms are quite diverse and even contradictory) are examined for insights into the purposes of secondary education and the directions needed for change. What will produce *an educated man* and what, indeed, will help students "develop the knowledge and skills they need to make sense out of their experience—their experience with themselves, with others, with the world—not just during adolescence, but for the rest of their lives"—are questions which need examination. (p. 336)

Student dissent coupled with legal action in some instances has been among the factors contributing to a growing ferment in high schools, leading to changes in three categories: a) minor changes aimed at creating a freer and more humane climate outside the classroom; b) more substantive changes aimed at humanizing the schools as a whole through freer schedules, different course requirements, and more independent study; and c) radical changes affecting the curriculum and the entire teaching-learning process.

Silberman has ITEMs illustrating each of these categories of changes. Flexible modular scheduling, free periods, increased independent study, alternatives to present grading practices and evaluation processes are described as first steps toward breaking "the repressive, almost prison-like atmosphere of most high schools," (p. 349) placing greater responsibility for learning on the student himself, including the way he learns. However, these changes merely skirt the need for basic reconsideration of what the high schools are for and for their rediscovering (or discovering?) their reasons for existing at all.

Among the handful of schools engaged in such more basic searches are Philadelphia's Parkway Program ("School without Walls"), Newton's Murray Road Annex, and Portland's Adams High School. Silberman discusses each of these "radical experiments" in some detail—suggesting risks and reservations as well as claims to gains. By its organization, Adams High represents two institutions in one—a comprehensive high school and a professional teacher education center. This arrangement is a significant one, Silberman concludes, observing: "Anyone concerned with reforming secondary education will want to watch the Adams High experiment with the closest interest and attention."(p. 369)

Education of the Teacher

In Part IV, Silberman comes back to the teacher—his qualities, his preparation, and, whatever educational technology is available, his indispensability. A thorough-going reform of teacher education is absolutely essential, Silberman argues, and the task is a formidable one since "it is not possible to reform the education of teachers without reforming higher education as a whole."(p. 374) Silberman reminds readers that almost three-fourths of the nation's colleges and universities are involved somehow in the preparation of teachers and that students, whether majoring in education or in an academic subject, take the bulk of their work (from two-thirds to three-fourths) in the academic departments. Thus, Silberman argues, if teachers "are poorly educated, it is the liberal arts professors, not just the educationists, who are to blame."(p. 377) His initial analysis focuses on the liberal education of teachers which he maintains should be a central purpose of all universities and colleges.

A beginning, he suggests, would involve incorporating "what the students are discovering for themselves into the curriculum—to make teaching a normal part of the undergraduate experience for every student, not just those who plan to teach."(p. 383) Such a step would represent a major step toward reforming education for all, representing a return to an older notion that "to be liberally educated is to be prepared to teach." Since that notion does little to clarify the meaning of *liberally educated,* Silberman examines alternate conceptions that have prevailed over the years, the debates which have been joined in the past decade or so, and the efforts to reconcile "the old tradition of liberal education and the new tradition of specialization in the disciplines . . . through an emphasis on the means of communication and the conduct and strategy of intellectual inquiry."(p. 408) Silberman notes that a growing number of colleges and universities are now asking basic questions about educational purposes and processes and that such lines of inquiry suggest "that we are at the beginning of a period of rich and thoughtful innovation in higher education."(p. 411) Perhaps.

A liberal education is, of course, a necessary but not sufficient condition for teacher education: teachers need professional education as well. Silberman looks at "The Teacher as Student: What's Wrong with Teacher Education" in some detail. He recounts the growth of normal schools to supply teachers for the mushrooming elementary and high school populations; the rift between the academicians and the educationists, "the unfortunate consequences of the educationists' isolation from the mainstream of academic life and the academicians' abdication of responsibility for teacher education;" (p. 430) the emergence of a "largely self-perpetuating educationist 'establishment' " of teacher trainers and schoolmen; the setting of certification requirements by this establishment; the "intellectual puerility" of education courses and especially the wasteland found in courses on methods of teaching.

Silberman notes that to the extent that teachers value any part of their professional education, it tends to be practice teaching— but even this aspect "is in as dismal a state as the rest of teacher education."(p. 452) Training in the process of interaction analysis and the use of micro-teaching techniques are cited as promising means for improving practice teaching. Silberman questions Conant's proposal that practice teaching be improved by having college supervisors of student teaching play a role "analogous to that of a clinical professor in certain medical schools."(p. 463) He has reservations about the medical school analogy, although he concurs that major changes in the social environment ("the invisible or informal curriculum" p. 469) must occur in the training of both doctors and teachers.

Relation of Teacher Education to Classroom

How *should* teachers be educated, then? Silberman opens his final chapter with the observation that "teacher education has suffered too long from too many answers and too few questions" and the warning that he has "no panacea or master plan to offer, and knows of none worth following."(p. 470) He notes that prospective teachers come to college with a rather firm idea of what teaching is about, having begun to form this image in kindergarten and first grade, and know all too well what most teachers do. What they need, Silberman says, are "alternative pictures of what teaching and learning can be, along with the techniques they need to implement them."(p. 471) Otherwise, new teachers simply do what they think teachers should be doing on the basis of their own observations and experiences. To understand and transmit such alternatives, faculties of education will have to revise their own conceptions of what and how they teach through development of new relationships with the public schools.

Silberman argues: "While the schools cannot be transformed unless colleges and universities turn out a new breed of teacher educated to think about purpose, the universities will be unable to do this unless they, working with schools, create classrooms that afford their students live models of what teaching can and should be."(p. 473)

The University of North Dakota's New School for Behavioral Studies in Education is cited approvingly as one possible model for such a new relationship, although its graduates are not *students of teaching* in the sense of having acquired "the grounding in theory or the intellectual disciplines they need in order to set their own goals or understand the reasons behind the teaching methods they use so competently."(p. 479) Despite this major shortcoming, New School faculty apparently use the same informal, individualized, non-directive approaches students are asked to adapt. Other examples of experimentation with informal approaches at the college and university level—courses, short-courses, workshops—are provided by Silberman, suggesting that this idea is central to his recommendations for teacher education reform.

Silberman returns to his plea for clarifying purpose, urging that teachers need more than a knowledge of subject matter combined with some student teaching: "They need knowledge *about* knowledge, about the ramifications of the subject or subjects they teach, about how those subjects relate to other subjects and to knowledge —and life—in general. They need insights into their purposes as a teacher—why they are teaching what they are teaching. . . ."(p. 489) Moreover, the prospective teacher needs help in understanding *himself* and this, Silberman suggests, "may actually be the most neglected aspect of teacher education."(p. 494) Some programs for helping to achieve such self-understanding are operative and these are described—counseling bordering on therapy, assessment-feedback counseling, T-groups, and sensitivity training.

Silberman observes that school administrators—superintendents, principals, guidance counselors, curriculum coordinators, and others—need the kind of education which focuses on defining purpose even more than the classroom teachers since they are in policy-determining roles. Finally, new programs for the preparation of college teachers and administrators are absolutely essential, ranging from modifications of existing Ph.D. programs to development of a separate teaching doctorate. Reappraisal and redesign of college curriculum, of relationships with various faculties within the college and university, of relationships between schools and colleges are necessary. The emphasis, Silberman concludes must shift from teaching to learning—"when schools become 'centers for inquiry' rather than buildings for the one-way transmission of information—teachers become learners along with their students; in Dewey's phrase, they become 'students of teaching.' "(p. 522)

How, then, shall Silberman's analysis and recommendations be judged? As a journalist, Silberman has done an excellent reporting job. He has observed, read, reflected, consulted and reported in a controlled, balanced fashion—outraged and indignant with much of what he has seen and yet quick to point out that schools are not a complete morass. His basic tenet is that whatever is wrong with the schools can be changed through reform which begins with clarification of educational purpose and that the education of teachers can spearhead educational reform. There can be serious question about this argument: schools exist in a larger societal context in which numerous social, political, economic, cultural, and moral forces have a direct impact on both the day-to-day operations as well as the long-term purposes of education and schooling. A major reservation concerning Silberman's book is precisely in his implication that if professionals and lay persons concern themselves with the basic questions of purpose, if consensus can be reached on what these purposes are, if the purposes are essentially humane—then all other elements of the educational process and of schooling will begin to fall into place. It is, of course, not that we have not been urged to shed our mindlessness before!

To the degree that the book is read as a basis for stimulating the kind of dialogue Silberman would encourage, the report will have served a useful purpose. Silberman's proposals for change are neither drastic nor surgical and, in fact, may suffer the fate of the various Conant reports—practitioners and public were able to convince themselves that they were already doing what was recommended or were moving in those directions. "The remaking of American education will not be possible without a new kind of public dialogue in which all interested parties join," Silberman concludes, but such dialogue must be a prelude to action— "all will have to act, which means that all will have to make difficult decisions; the road to reform is always uphill."(p. 524)

Taken on these terms, the Silberman book should serve a very useful purpose at this juncture of American educational history. Those who seek a blueprint for reforming either schools or the education of teachers will not find more than a way of approaching the problem of reform.

Notes

1. James S. Coleman, et al., *Equality of Educational Opportunity* (Washington, D.C.: U.S. Government Printing Office, 1966).
2. Arthur R. Jensen, "How Much Can We Boost IQ and Scholastic Achievement?", *Harvard Educational Review*, Winter 1969, pp. 1-123.

II

The Greening of the Schools

James D. Koerner

"Half the truth," says Poor Richard, "is often a great lie." With reluctance I have to say that Mr. Silberman has told us half the truth about American schools and has thereby limned a portrait of them in which they appear much uglier than they are. His proposal for making them instantly beautiful seems to me equally far from reality. I say this with regret because my hopes were high for this book and because there is still much in it to applaud. But it is fundamentally ill-conceived.

The premise upon which Silberman's long volume is based is the simple contention, stated early and reiterated often, that American schools are "grim, joyless places."(p. 10) From that unqualified assertion flows the rest of the book. Since I can accept neither his premise nor the miracle pill he prescribes, I must try to rebut his main contention.

But how does one counter such a peremptory argument? Presumably not by offering evidence to show that schools are happy, free, and joyful places. Quantities of such evidence could be gathered if one had a few years in which to work, a staff to help, and a large grant. But it would no doubt be *evidence* of the same type offered by Silberman: flamboyant *items* listed in a supposedly objective fashion, the suggestion being that they are representative samples, when they might be quite extraordinary samples if not caricatures; innumerable statements by administrators, professors of education, and sundry observers of schools, but few by practicing teachers; and voluminous quotations from the writings of psychologists, philosophers, and assorted theoreticians with whom one agrees.

The trouble with such evidence alleging that joy and happiness are widespread in schools is that the reader would be helpless to evaluate it, and of necessity would be thrown back on his personal experience. So it is with Silberman's book. What else can one do but accept it on faith or reject it on the basis of what one considers common sense? No firm evidence appears in the book for or against Silberman's principal claims and theories. What appears are anecdotes, impressions, beliefs, assertions, and points of view. All of which would be fair enough if the author were merely making a statement of position about our problems. But the book is represented as a searching analytical study of "the crisis in the classroom." That, it is not.

Perhaps all one can do is to offer opinions contrary to Silberman's opinions. My opinion is that American schools are better than Silberman thinks. They may be a long way this side of paradise but they are, taken collectively the way Silberman takes them, a long way beyond the purgatory in which he claims to find them. That some of them are in some degree grim, repressive, and joyless hardly needs saying. Who doubts it? But a hundred thousand schools and a couple of million teachers are not to be sweepingly indicted as "killers of the dream."(p. 10) Things are a bit more complicated than that.

The attitude of most people toward schools depends on what they expect a mammoth system of universal education to be able to achieve at this point in history. Many find the educational system performing more or less to their satisfaction. Many, possibly a majority, are dissatisfied in one degree or another. For members of the latter group, it is a question of how far short the system falls of their goals that determines whether they are educational revolutionaries, reformers, or mild meliorists. For Silberman the schools are failing so catastrophically to meet his particular set of goals that only revolutionary change would be equal to "the crisis." Like Charles A. Reich, another visionary idol and idolater of the youth culture, Silberman has nothing less in mind than the greening of the schools; after which, and because of which, will come the greening of America, thereby creating what Silberman describes most often simply as a "humane" society.

For readers who have a passing acquaintance with utopian literature in education, there must be a certain ennui, a pronounced sense of *déjà vu*, that sets in early in the book. Echoes assault the ears from every page. Here is Comenius without the metaphors or the religious foundation for his theory; here is Rousseau without the learning, the limpid style, or the truly arresting thought; here is William Heard Kilpatrick under some restraint; here are gaggles of old-time progressives slightly toughened (lifting barbells instead of marshmallows); here above all is John Dewey, in English. And here too are dozens of our militant new progressives demanding in

stentorian tones that schools and men be kinder and happier than
they are—by order of the commanding officer. Indeed the inquisi-
tor, who so often walks beside the utopian, is not altogether absent
from Silberman's book. Here and there, even in the inspirational
passages, one senses the sermonizing shade of Savonarola, with a
mailed fist.

Everyone, of course, is for the humane society. The problem is
how to get there from here. However we do it, the road will be a
lot longer and more tortuous than anything dreamt of in Silberman's philosophy. Meanwhile, schools have a more limited job
to do than to take on the total reconstruction of society. Hence, my
dissatisfaction with the existing educational system is less uncompromising than Silberman's. It is acute but not apocalyptic. I
am willing to settle for more immediate and specific reforms than
is Silberman, who has the splendid audacity to subtitle his book,
The Remaking of American Education. No shrinking violet,
he—not one to be intimidated by the challenge of providing answers for the problems of an eighty-billion-dollar-a-year industry
that consumes the full-time attention of at least one out of every
four Americans.

I look at the educational system and see the glass half-full rather
than half-empty. I see a system that provides more education for
more people than any other in the world's history. I see a system
more open, more flexible, and more generous than that of any
other nation. I see a system full of flaws having mostly to do with
confusion of purpose and the tormented problems of sheer mass.
But between revolution and reform, I unhesitatingly opt for the
latter. So when I encounter accusations of universal failure in the
educational system and in society, I remind myself that they can be
true only in the sense that man himself is a *failure.* That is a proposition that takes one into metaphysical speculation.

Silberman on Primary Schools

Having stated my disagreement with the main premise of Silberman's book, let me turn more specifically to his three-part discussion of primary, secondary, and professional education. His
treatment of the informal infant and primary school in England
seems to me as imbalanced as his discussion of the elementary
school in the United States. He is as adulatory of the one as he is
condemnatory of the other. Just as I do not believe the American
elementary school is in such desperate straits as he does, I do not
believe the informal English school is the embodiment of the good,
the true, and the beautiful for all to see and emulate.

A great many American elementary schools are as *free* as anything in England. Far from being obsessed with what in the trade is called the cognitive at the expense of the affective, they are regarded by many people, especially parents, as entirely too permissive and undirected. I don't know how many primary schools Silberman visited in the United States, but he cannot have found a very representative sample if he did not see many, owing nothing to England, with happy children and freedom in abundance (although how much education goes on in them may be another question).

Silberman's comparisons between English and American schools are frequently too naive to be taken seriously. Here is a typical instance:

What impresses an American the most . . . (about the English primary school) is the combination of great joy and spontaneity and activity with equally great self-control and order. The joyfulness is pervasive; in almost every classroom visited, virtually every child appeared happy and engaged. One simply does not see bored or restless or unhappy youngsters, or youngsters with the glazed look so common in American schools.(p. 228)

Whether visitors to American elementary schools find large numbers of students walking around in a glaze I don't know, but I feel pretty sure that such massive simplifications as Silberman indulges in do not reflect the reality of either school system. Oscar Wilde once remarked that the truth is rarely pure and never simple. I find Silberman's *truth* consistently too pure and simple for the real world.

The Leicestershire experiment may be an advance in elementary schooling—people in Leicestershire will readily tell an American visitor that they got all of their ideas from the United States—but to make an intelligent judgment about it, we need to know a great deal more than we learn through Silberman's tourist-eyed view of the matter. What evidence of success does he present for the English primary school? He relies mostly on a sort of impressionistic litmus paper ritually applied to determine whether children appear joyful, happy, and content. One hopes, although the hope may be misplaced, that American educators need grounds more relevant than this for importing what is still an experiment in a minority of English schools.

Well, says Silberman, the reading ability of the children in these schools appears at least not to suffer. Also, certain studies, although they do not "provide enough information . . . to enable a reader to draw his own conclusions about the adequacy of the controls," (p. 260) show the advantages of the informal school. And anyhow, we probably "look in the wrong places" to find the evidence of success; we should be looking not at academic attainment but at "how children feel about themselves, about school, and about learning."(p. 262) American schoolmen might have a tough time selling that spongy standard to parents.

I see no way in which Silberman's readers, without better information than he provides, can assess his central argument about the superiority of the English primary school. Lacking such knowledge, many readers are likely to feel, as I do, that the children of England's informal primary school would probably score about the same as their counterparts in the United States or most other Western countries on such dubious questions as how they "feel about themselves, about school, and about learning." For their part the English themselves are not universally enchanted with the informal school. If one is to judge by the British press, there are more than a few parents as well as educators thoroughly unhappy with the informal approach. Far from regarding it as a high-quality item for export, they are warning of disaster at home and pressing for . . . guess what, the reform of the informal primary school.

It is a basic and regrettable deficiency of the American school system that it offers the public so little choice in types of schools, especially elementary schools. Most American parents have no choice but to send their young children to the neighborhood school, whatever its philosophy and pedagogical ethos, if either can be clearly determined. Even if they send their children across town, the chances of their finding a different type of school are slim. How to provide genuine alternatives in the educational system is a major problem that the nation has not begun to solve.

If individual elementary schools did have to stand for something and to compete for the allegiance of parents with schools that stood for something else, we would have at least one compelling means of assessing different approaches to education. Schools adopting one or another variation of the informal English approach would have a chance to compete in a free market with formal schools and others in between. If the English approach were everything Silberman says it is, its superiority would presumably become evident and would command the patronage of a majority of parents, leaving schools of a different philosophy for the minority who preferred them.

That kind of pluralism in elementary schools will be a long time coming, if it ever does. In the meantime we have only primitive means for testing out sharply different approaches to elementary education. Thus I can take no comfort in the possibility that a neoprogressive movement, which is all Silberman is really talking about, may be inflicted on a widespread scale on parents who have no choice in the matter. That this is precisely what may happen is strongly suggested by the appetite for fads and the frequency of bandwagons that has characterized the educational system since the First World War. If we could have a limited amount of carefully designed experimentation with the English approach, voluntary for the parents involved, one could hardly object. But Silberman's prescription admits of nothing so modest. He has seen the future and it works. He makes clear that nothing short of an overhaul of the whole educational system will do.

Silberman on High Schools

When Silberman turns to the high school, on which he spends less than half the space he does on the primary school, his case seems even less persuasive. He begins with a blanket indictment of the customary sort:

. . . secondary schools tend to be even more authoritarian and repressive than elementary schools; the values they transmit are the values of docility, passivity, conformity, and lack of trust.(p. 324)

A little later Silberman speaks of the "repressive [the era's most fashionable adjective, it seems], almost prison-like atmosphere of most high schools."(p. 349) I find such canonical assertions no easier to accept about the secondary school than about the elementary school. High schools transmit all kinds of values and I doubt that Silberman's are the chief ones. Even if they are, his uncritical discussion of the three avant-garde schools that he claims are doing something about it is entirely unconvincing. As he acknowledges himself, none of these schools can yet be called a success. The experiments are still too new and are surrounded with too many special conditions.

Silberman's chapter on the high school does contain a good discussion of the substance of a secondary education. Fortunately, he does not share the attitude of such romantic seers and prophets as Edgar Friedenberg, John Holt, and George Leonard, for whom any subject is as good as any other and maybe no preordained subjects are best of all. Silberman has more respect for our intellectual and cultural heritage. He wants an education in basic subjects in high school carried out along progressive lines, although it is not at all clear that this is what happens in the three schools he admires. He places a major emphasis on aesthetic education—art, music, dance, and cites the failure of Arthur Bestor and others, including myself, to share this emphasis. I accept his position with reservations and agree on the potential importance of these subjects. However, I would hope that the study of them would move beyond the express-yourself-do-your-thing stage in which it often gets mired. High school students in this culture are not exactly starved for free-wheeling, self-indulgent self-expression.

Silberman apparently found nothing in the highly structured English secondary school to recommend to Americans. One wonders what happens to the liberated children coming out of the English lower schools when they reach the secondary institutions, which are more rigid in every respect, far more so in Scotland and Wales, than American schools. Nor would he have found anything to recommend to us in the secondary schools of Germany, France, Italy, Switzerland, or Japan, and least of all in the Communist countries. In other words, none of the world's industrialized nations, which are the only ones that can finance universal education of 10, 12, or more years, would agree with Silberman's approach to secondary education.

They could be wrong and he could be right. But the only evidence for it, apart from Silberman's personal convictions and his copious quotations from others, is what he finds happening with a small number of very special students at three experimental high schools. And even that, he acknowledges, is not yet very clear. Yet he entitles this chapter, "Reforming the High School." It seems to me that any reform-minded schoolman would look in vain for something to help him in this painfully inconclusive and pretentious chapter.

Silberman on Teacher Education

The final third of Silberman's book deals with what he calls "the education of educators." I found it frustrating. He says all the right things about the sad state of teacher training, the dead hand of the professional establishment, the dreary teaching in many of the liberal arts departments, etc. Incontestable. And worth having said again. But the section suffers from two deficiencies. First, there are grievous gaps in the discussion. Second, he offers pitifully few remedies or recommendations for what he deplores.

As is true of the earlier sections of the book, Silberman in this section slights the secondary school. He discusses the liberal education of all teachers taken together, which is good up to a point. However, there are also vital differences in preparation between a secondary and an elementary teacher, but Silberman either does not think so or declines to deal with them. More puzzling still is his nearly complete neglect of the wide world of graduate education. I mean the burgeoning business that produces master's and doctor's of education by the tens of thousands who later occupy positions of leadership in education. If public schools are as bad as Silberman says they are, he really ought to have looked at the education of people who have had a lot to do with making them that way—

those who take advanced degrees in education. Out of 525 pages, Silberman spends about three in a generalized discussion of what is wrong with graduate programs in education! James Bryant Conant made the same incomprehensible decision in his book on teacher education, thereby ignoring a problem that was central to everything else he discussed.

Again, a reform minded teacher of teachers, looking for something to take away from this section of the book, would find little. Silberman describes Vito Perrone's New School in North Dakota, which is chiefly concerned with elementary teachers, and gives a brief description of a few other programs and practices he likes. These experimental efforts, like his three experimental high schools, are accorded nothing like the analytical treatment they deserve if so much weight is to be put on them.

The formless and unfocused discussion that occurs in the final third of the book makes a disappointing peroration for a long volume that finds so much fundamentally wrong in schools and colleges and that indicates with such certitude that the author knows some better ways of conducting education. In a word, the final section, which one might suppose would be the strongest, is the weakest. It offers little guidance to those in charge of the education of educators beyond telling them again what their problems are.

Silberman is dead right about one thing: the prevalence of what he calls mindlessness in American education. Throughout the book he puts an admirable stress on the importance of conscious, continuing thought about the purposes of education. He finds little of it going on now at any level of the educational system, and he is right. I don't share his faith in college courses in the history and philosophy of education, much less in the sociology of education. He seems to feel that such courses have the power to force questions of philosophy and purpose into the consciousness of teachers and educators. That may be true when such courses are in the hands of gifted professors. But they are not in such hands most of the time, and they are consequently among the most deadly of all required courses in a teacher's preparation. Why endorse them as a means of combating mindlessness when they are so often mindless themselves, and when there is little prospect of their being taught well to the majority of future educators? Still, it would be nothing but a gain if educators would think as seriously and insistently about the goals and purposes of education as Silberman urges.

Parents and Education

A couple of nagging doubts remain concerning the general character of the book. One has to do with parental rights and expectations. The record is abundantly clear that most parents do not become dissatisfied with the educational system because they don't find schools flexible, free, or joyous enough. Parents get unhappy when they think schools are too permissive and undisciplined, and when schools fail to teach children to read and figure. Most of the educational controversies of the last quarter-century have found parents, including those in the inner cities, on the side of order, rigor, and systematic instruction in basic subjects—formalism, if you like. Now comes Silberman proclaiming that "the remedy for the defects of slum schools is the remedy for the defects of all schools; namely, to transform them into free, open, humane, and joyous institutions."(p. 62)

The American public, having financed the most gigantic educational enterprise in the history of man, may prefer a different set of priorities from Silberman's. They may feel that public schools need a less nebulous, more measurable set of goals. In that case it is the parents' priorities that ought to prevail. Educators have traditionally had little faith in the wisdom of parents, and intellectuals even less so. But I submit that when the issues are clearly drawn in public education, parental desires should take precedence over those of educators. The problem, of course, is that the issues are not clearly drawn in Silberman's book, for who is going to argue that schools should *not* be humane and happy places? The question is whether parents agree that a primary, indeed a relentless, emphasis on freedom and joy will produce the results claimed by Silberman. I feel pretty sure that most parents would not agree; and their view, not that of journalists or other commentators, should dominate.

The other question, the obverse side of the first one, has to do with how much faith parents have in the wisdom of educators. If educators bear the main responsibility, as Silberman suggests, for the present condition of the schools, why would anyone suppose that they have the ability to remake the system, even with the somewhat remote help of philosophers and social engineers? Moreover, what is there to suggest that educators have either the right or the wisdom to decide what society's goals should be and how schools can make these goals possible?

Silberman says that our greatest educational problem is "not how to increase efficiency of the schools; it is how to create and maintain a humane society."(p. 203) Quite a few people are apt to think, as I do, that schools, certainly in a mass system of universal education that will soon take in fifty million students, have a more modest and a more specific function to perform. Laymen are also apt to be profoundly distrustful, as I am, of the Messianic impulse in educators. They are apt to feel that educators have no more insight into what makes a humane society than anyone else has. And laymen, when they find themselves face to face with the vanities and overweening ambitions of schoolmasters who are bent on remaking schools and then society according to their private visions, are apt to put up some stout resistance—thank God.

III

The Cheerful Crisis

John S. Mann

Crisis in the Classroom is a big book; it covers an enormously broad range of topics. It is an odd book in that with the left hand it spins out a hair-raising tale of mis-education, and then with the right hand calmly, indeed cheerfully, reminds us that no one really means any harm, that good education is going on here and there and that if we only begin to think seriously about purpose, things will fall into place. Silberman tells us he is indignant. Perhaps he is. But the indignation is only apparent in the introduction. And, more alarming, the book is utterly devoid of anxiety, of worry. This makes me very anxious.

Still the book is important, or can be if we read it carefully, skeptically, and questioningly. In this commentary, I do not try to *cover* the entire book. I only try to share my responses to those aspects of the book that most strongly captured my attention.

Mindlessness—Purpose

In spite of its breadth, the book is cogently organized around a clear and sustained point-of-view which is also its thesis:

Schools fail . . . because of mindlessness. (p. 81)

The moral purpose [is] universal and dominant in all instruction . . . (p. 9) [quoted from Dewey]

[the solution] must lie in infusing the various educating institutions with purpose, more important, with thought about purpose and about the ways in which techniques, content, and organization fulfill or alter purpose. (p. 11) [the teacher-educator] must be educated to self-scrutiny and to serious thought about purpose . . . (p. 374)

Everything in the book flows between the two poles, mindlessness and purpose. The thesis: Where and inasmuch as schooling is bad, it is mindless. Where and inasmuch as schooling is good, it is purposeful. This apposition of *mindless* and *purpose* struck me as curious at first. But then I came to understand that *purpose* for Silberman is a very intellectual phenomenon. Not narrowly intellectual, as is implied by the quotation from Robert M. Hutchins ("A human being acts in a human way if he thinks," p. 7) but intellectual in a sense that reflects the integration of feeling, thinking, and acting. "The ancient Hebrews understood this well; the Biblical verb *yadah,* 'to know,' signifies a unification of intellect, feeling, and action. . ."(p. 8)

Mindlessness is ". . . the failure to think seriously and deeply about purpose." (p. 11) And purpose is philosophy:

The central task of teacher education, therefore, is to provide teachers with a sense of purpose, or, if you will, with a philosophy of education. This means developing teachers' ability to think seriously, deeply, and continuously about the purposes and consequences of what they do. . . . (p. 472).

So after a while the apposition becomes familiar and understandable. But not unproblematic. Questions arise like *Whose* purpose? and what about conflicting purposes? Silberman has the liberal's humanistic faith that if people would only think seriously they would all turn out to want the same thing, or at least to have compatible purposes. (1) I do not share that faith. I think that much, though not all, of the strife that we are experiencing now derives from fundamentally conflicting purposes that cannot be reduced by serious thought. Silberman does not deal with conflict of purpose. This is why he can be so optimistic, and it is why I cannot be so optimistic.

Silberman Is Deweyan . . . and More

The relation between mind and purpose that Silberman sees is Deweyan in a fundamental way (cf. especially Dewey on the *end-in-view*). But Silberman stops short of exploring this fully. He sees that a teacher must be a learner and that his learning occurs by virtue of his sense of purpose (throughout part IV), and he sees that the teacher's sense of purpose is a critical variable in the lives of his students. But he does not unequivocally identify the function of purpose in the education of school-children. He does best with this in connection with his discussion of two high-schools—the Murray Road Annex (pp. 356-364) and the John Adams High School (pp. 364-369). Here he sees the importance of the dialectic between *purpose* and *freedom* in transcending the vacuous debate over structure or non-structure ("discovering that freedom is more than the absence of restraint, and developing the self-discipline that would enable them to use their freedom, were slow and sometimes painful processes."(p.558). But he treats this somewhat as an important epiphenomenon rather than as the problem around which almost all other curriculum problems revolve.

That he does so is clearly evident on page 367 when he accepts Robert Schwartz's view of the *intellectual bankruptcy* of the *bull session*. Not that the *bull session* is an acceptable final form for educational discourse. Rather, he overlooks, or at least fails to note, what any educator who has worked with students in a *free school* environment will recognize: that the *bull session* is a critical transitional stage in the process from mindlessly accepting the mindlessness of a school system to discovering and acting upon one's own sense of purpose. It is a stage that must be returned to from time to time for the purpose of rerooting oneself in genuine problems between the times when tasks are clear and dominant. The stage cannot become entrenched. But neither can it be by passed or its recurrent transitional importance overlooked. A small point, but one that, like his discussion of *grades*, shows Silberman stopping just short of the mark.

In his earlier discussion of elementary schools, Silberman does a wonderful job of examining Robert K. Merton's hypothesis of the *self-fulfilling prophecy* and the research on the relation of teacher expectation to student performance, all in the context of portraying the phenomenal things that lone isolated educators in the United States can do with thoughtful and well-informed purposefulness. But he does not consider the very complex problems of purposefulness in the lives of the elementary students. He seems more or less to accept the view that it is sufficient for that age-group to simply absorb purpose from the teacher. Do we wish to accept that view? *Purpose* must have a developmental dimension to it, which must have something to do, in the fashion of Maslow, with the emergence of drives that transcend the *primary instincts*. What is the relation between the acceptance of purpose from teacher and the emergence of personal purposiveness? Not a simple one, probably. Sometimes the latter might inhibit the former, sometimes facilitate it. Another factor is the social group, another the home culture, and yet another the general social-historical factors discussed by all the people between *The Lonely Crowd* and *The Greening of America.* Does anyone know anything about this?

To repeat, the relation Silberman sees between mind and purpose is Deweyan. But he falls short of drawing out the full pedagogical implications. He's best when he's dealing with the education of teachers. At the other levels, he has cut out some work for us. So did Dewey.

And Silberman is Deweyan in other ways, too. He advocates a progressive *use* of subject matter, and not a Progressivist *abolition* of subject matter. He frequently, though not with complete consistency, sees *interaction* as the key process rather than *instruction*; "The educator's task is to maximize the occasion," he says, quoting an English informal school headmaster (p. 238), to which he adds: "It is more than that. The teacher does not just maximize the occasion; he makes the occasion possible in the first place by the kind of environment he creates and maintains."(p. 238)

In *Democracy and Education,* Dewey said that "we never educate directly, only indirectly by means of the environment."

He understands the function of interest in a Deweyan sense, too:

. . . since children have no inborn impulse to read, school must create an environment that will evoke it, that will make them *want* to read and write . . . But first the child must be comfortable with language. Hence children are encouraged to talk, to communicate with each other and the adults around them about the things that interest and engage them. The incredible richness and variety of stuff in the classroom and the great diversity of activities going on at once provide that encouragement. Indeed, in an environment in which so many people are doing so many different things, communication almost becomes a necessity . . . (p. 241)

And yet I'm not entirely satisfied to say that Silberman is Deweyan. It may be best to say that he leaves us with very much the same sorts of problems Dewey left us with. From my own viewpoint this is equivalent to saying that he directs our attention away from both the trivial (the behavioral objectives movement) and the colossal (computer-assisted instruction) blind alleys we spend our own time and the public's money upon, into a recognition of the genuinely problematic in education.

An Incomplete Educational Vision

Yet I'm not quite satisfied with that statement either; in subtle ways Silberman seems to not quite grasp the significance of the problems he has pointed to. Why, for example, does he fall just short of dealing adequately with the relation between freedom, discipline, and structure in his discussion of Murray Roads Annex? Why does he not quite see beyond Robert Schwartz's dichotomous view of the problem:

Schwartz's hope is that students and teachers will move from the problems that evoke their interest to a study of the intellectual disciplines needed to illuminate and deal with them—that the general education course, in short, will have serious intellectual content.(p. 307)

Why, after a nice critique of Arthur Bestor and James Koerner, does he continue:

This is in no way to suggest, however, that any one piece of learning is as good as any other, and that high school students therefore might just as well study whatever interests them. Knowing one thing is *not* the same as knowing another, and some things are more worth knowing than others. Surely a man cannot be considered educated unless he has some understanding of Science.(p. 333)

Silberman seems in all of these instances to be operating out of a fundamentally conservative view of epistemology and of schooling. Epistemologically what he wishes to conserve is the classical dichotomy between objective and subjective views of knowledge, and his own affinity to the objective view. Schoolwise, what he wishes to conserve is the notion that school is a place where the student is brought into contact with the sort of knowledge that is held to be objective. His humane approach to schooling consists principally in recognizing and respecting the fact that students have subjectivity, but the *task* of schooling is still to engage them in the objectivity of knowledge. For this reason, his treatment of all the topics related to the Deweyan notion of interest has a certain shallowness to it. For indeed if the subjective-objective dichotomy is held to be true, then *interest* belongs to the *subjective* realm, and the most progressive thing one can do with it is to use it as a springboard to the objective (which is precisely what Schwartz is talking about) . . . instead of ignoring or suppressing it.

It is not clear to me whether Dewey, whose constant theme was the transcendence of classical dichotomies, got over this one or not. (His "Pattern of Inquiry," which I do not yet understand well, and certain sections of *Human Nature and Conduct,* strongly suggest that he did.) It *is* clear to me, though, that the Deweyan concept of interest—and a great number of related concepts such as *activity, inquiry,* and *creativity*—becomes enormously enriched and clarified when it is viewed in the context of an epistemology that does transcend the subjective-objective dichotomy. My point is to exemplify the proposition that Silberman does not quite grasp the significance of the problems he has pointed to. The example chosen is a critical one, I think, because the objectivist view of knowledge which Silberman holds is fundamental to almost all current thinking about schooling however humane, and it constitutes the fundamental barrier to a cogent understanding of the function in education of a whole set of concepts that cluster around the Deweyan notion of *interest*.

Optimism Is Not Enough

The first half of *Crisis in the Classroom* is laced with "we can do it, boys" pep talk. It is a sincere optimism, in spite of the pep-talk phrases. Optimism pervades the book. It is appealing. But I do not find it persuasive.

It is to Silberman's credit, I believe, that he resists the temptation to give any pat prescriptions for success. He is most keenly aware that good education happens when a complex combination of things lines up the right way, and that the alignment is too complex to be mechanically engineered with some gimmickry. . . . I think, unfortunately, that his argument *is* basically simplistic, to wit: in order to have good education in the schools we need to have well-educated teachers. In order to have well-educated teachers, we need to have well-educated teachers of teachers who can thoughtfully, purposively and wisely educate teachers. And where do these come from? Silberman appears to believe that we professors of education, assisted by a new spirit of cooperation from our liberal arts colleagues, being reminded of our collective mindlessness can and will simply shake the dust from our shoulders and become thoughtful and purposeful. Saying we can do this strikes me as not much different from saying that Napoleon could have retreated from Russia before his army froze to death. And saying we *will*—preposterous. Not a shred of evidence.

That's my gut response to Silberman's optimism. But let me back off and be more thoughtful. Silberman does not actually say precisely that we just *will* shake the dust from our shoulders. And he does present some kind of evidence on behalf of his optimism.

He does say they are doing it in England, and on a fairly massive scale. He gives a sufficiently ample and clear picture of the English model so that without being able precisely to label it, we end up with a fair understanding of what he means by good education. Then he goes on to show that here and there good education is going on in the United States. The number of outposts of good education is rapidly increasing, he argues, and points to the

growing demand for programs like Lillian Weber's and Lore Rasmussen's, and to the expanding desire, evidenced at the University
of Connecticut, to learn from the English model. Let's look more
closely at this evidence.

Silberman begins the thematically central seventh chapter, "It
Can Happen Here," by considering whether the English model he
has just reported upon in the previous chapter depends upon the
teachers involved possessing extraordinary skill, sensitivity, and
energy. . . . "If the success of informal education were due to
the fact that English primary teachers are a superior breed—then
the approach would not be likely to work in the United States, at
least not on a large enough scale to be significant."(p. 206)

He goes on to assert that such is not the case, and presents two
concise arguments.

1) English primary teachers are not a superior breed; on the contrary,
they come from much the same background as do American teachers.
Some 40% of English female primary school teachers, for example,
have fathers who are blue-collar workers, and more than half come
from lower-middle-class backgrounds; as in the United States, teaching
is an important avenue of social mobility, and has been for a long
time.(p. 266)

The relevance of this argument depends upon the correctness of
the rather startling assumption that "extraordinary skill, sensitivity, and energy" are associated with "good breeding," that is, with
parentage in some class higher than blue-collar or lower-middle.
This Jensenism is neither documented nor explicated. I assume it
to be false, and thus dismiss the argument.

2) English primary school teachers tend to be younger and less experienced than their American counterparts, for teacher turnover,
especially in infant schools, is extraordinarily high.(p. 266-267)

Silberman documents this plausible proposition adequately, and
concludes that "the success of informal schooling cannot be at-
tributed to extraordinary talent or experience on the part of English teachers."(p. 267) But the argument is fallacious in two re-
spects. First, the turnover and attrition rates cited are for *all* English
primary school teachers and not just for those engaged in the new
informal education. It is entirely plausible that the turnover rate in
the schools Silberman has reported on as exemplifying good education do *not* have an appreciably higher turnover or attrition rate
than U.S. schools.

Second, even assuming that the turnover and attrition rates *are*
appreciably higher in the schools in question; one *can* conclude

that the teachers are not extraordinarily *experienced*, but one *cannot* conclude that the teachers do not possess extraordinary talent (skill, sensitivity, energy). There are many conditions under which less experienced teachers might well have a greater talent pool. Their training may have been more recent. The status of the profession may have been higher when the less experienced entered the profession. The necessity to survive in a bureaucratic school system might tend to *extinguish* talent, so that talent could actually tend toward varying *inversely* with experience.

These are the only concrete arguments Silberman musters against the contention that the English primary teachers in the informal schools possess superior talents, and consequently that the "approach would not be likely to work in the United States . . . ."

By contrast: "I met the kind of people I had never met before —human beings of a very high order."(p. 278)

This from an HMI describing his first contact with the people involved in informal schooling. Clearly, Silberman's argument against the *extraordinary teacher* hypothesis is inconclusive.

The case for optimism does not really rest on this narrow point, though the point is by no means trivial. Silberman has carefully, thoroughly, and with what strikes me as a fair measure of objectivity, documented and portrayed a number of apparently successful efforts in this country to establish thoughtful, purposeful and effective educational programs. And it is indeed heartening and impressive to see all the very splendid efforts one has heard about here and there laid out side by side. The sum is greater than I would have guessed it to be. The question before us, though, is whether Silberman's repeated affirmation that "it can happen here"—"it" being solidly purposeful and thoughtful education on a mass scale—is a reasonable expectation or a "consumation devoutly to be wished for" but, really, rather unlikely.

It is clear that we have working among us a devoted, courageous, and effective, but very very small army of outstanding educators: Martha Froelich, Marie Hughes, Lillian Weber, Lore Rasmussen, Vito Perrone, and perhaps a dozen more. It is apparently true that these people are getting results, and much more important results than a mere boost in reading achievement scores—fundamental educational results. The question is whether their results *depend* precisely on their very extraordinary talents, or whether a movement, given impetus by these talents, is likely to take root where the talents are more ordinary. The question is not how many more programs can Lillian Weber run, but rather how far the quality will spread beyond the reach of her direct energies, and how much will the quality deteriorate with increased distance and time. For surely it is an idle hope to think we are likely soon to have enough Lillian Webers to go around. The answer will take such forms as a fair assessment of the schools in the "Follow Through" program of the United States Office of Education and of the effectiveness of the young teaching interns working with Dr. Vincent R. Rogers at Connecticut as they filter out into public school systems. These kinds of assessments necessarily lie in the future. There is yet a case to be made for optimism.

A Case Against Optimism

There is another way to look at things. To the question "why do you think it will work" one can always answer "why not?" There are, unfortunately, several strong, though not conclusive, answers. First, there is the obvious fact that this generation of reformers is preceded by other brilliant educators who have failed to affirmatively effect education beyond their own immediate sphere of influence. Something seems always to happen to the best ideas in American education: the further they get from their source the stronger the vacuous and the faddish and the weaker the cogent and substantive components of reform become. As excellent an educator as John Goodlad, Silberman reminds us, has seen his very clear, simple and educationally-sound conceptions become increasingly farcical as they spread beyond his direct influence.(p. 167-68) Dr. Weber already has qualms about her *approach* spreading too fast.(p. 487) The substitution of fad for substance is no stranger to American education, and I see little reason to expect anything different this time around. The bandwagon, indeed, has already begun to roll.

Second, the English informal schools flourish under an administrative system which gives them a good deal more protection from the political and commercial expediencies which make a veritable ping-pong ball of our schools.

Third, there is the overwhelming lawfulness of bureaucracy. With utter certainty bureaucracies resist any change that threatens their continuity. Nothing is more clear than the proposition that widespread adaptation of anything like the English informal schooling would require massive reordering of structures which lie at the heart of the school bureaucracy's self-protective mechanism. This is made amply clear when he discusses the John Adams high school in detail. The argument is not weakened any by consideration of the fact that the most far-reaching successful reform seems to be taking place in a state which for a variety of reasons is among the least bureaucratized in the nation.

And fourth, and perhaps both most important and most difficult for me to state convincingly: the mindlessness is not all that mindless, the evil not all that benign, and the oppressiveness that characterizes our schools not all that accidental. John Holt is glib, no doubt, in his vision of teachers as conspirators against children. But Silberman is equally glib, I think, in his denial that the badness of schooling has any systemic or intentional dimensions at all.

I think it foolish in the extreme to deny that much of our current schooling practice derives explicitly from the intent of various commerical and political interests, as well as from the private visions, commitments, and purposes of educators who do not share Mr. Silberman's humanism. Can it honestly be said that no one who has participated in the mad rush to the suburbs intended to have their tax money go into better schools for their kids and the kids of other affluent families at the expense of the relatively poor people left down town? Can it honestly be said that, having got to the prized suburbs, the affluent have not knowingly substituted the passing on of class privilege via college admissions for any serious educational purpose to schooling? Can it honestly be asserted that the craze for science at the expense of a more balanced approach to curriculum reform was a mindless accident rather than the intent of influential politicians, scientists, and corporations? I think not. I won't enumerate other similar instances, of which there are a great many.

The point here is that what goes on in our schools is as much the result of shrewd intent as it is the result of mindlessness. The intent, of course, is rarely the overt intent to treat children destructively. But the system required to serve certain interests *is* in fact destructive of children, and the fact that we have such a system at the very best reflects a perverse sense of priorities. There are indeed many teachers and administrators who struggle valiantly to make their schools humane, but clearly there are also those who have chosen to have, and will continue to choose to have, a system more closely resembling the realities Silberman disparages than the hope he professes. They will tidy the system up a bit, make it more efficient, to be sure. They will legitimize it with liberal rhetoric, much of which will come right from Silberman's book.

There is, then, a case *against* optimism, as well as a fair number of gaps in the case *for* optimism. While the intent of Silberman's insistent repetition that we can do it is undoubtedly to spur us on, I fear he doesn't yet know the educator's capacity for complacence. All we need to keep us from ever looking seriously at the question of purpose, or any other question, is someone from the sidelines pointing optimistically to our however widely dispersed successes.

Perhaps we *can* do it. But the odds are heavy, and at best it will take a lot more than deep thought about purpose. It will take a long, bitter, messy, and not always clearly righteous political struggle for which few of us have either appetite or courage or skill.

The Importance of History

From the first page of the Foreward (p. vii) on, it is clear that Silberman wants his book to make a difference in how we conduct education. He wants it to figure in the world of educational events. He is speaking as an educational reformer, and he is "speaking to laymen and professionals alike" in their roles as potential educational reformers. For this reason, among others, his chapter on "The Failure of Educational Reform" (Chapter 5) is a particularly important one. The history of educational reform is not all failure. But if an assessment of current schooling is the proper criterion by which to make a general judgement, that history [might be viewed as] one of . . . failure. What is most important to note in Silberman's treatment of the failure of reform, and what Silberman portrays especially poignantly in the particular case of Jerrold Zacharias, is the failure of the reformers to locate themselves historically. He writes:

. . . the reformers by and large ignored the experience of the past . . . they were therefore unaware of the fact that almost everything they said had been said before, by Dewey, Whitehead, Bode, Rugg, etc., and they were unaware that almost everything they tried to do had been tried before . . . (p. 179)

The result was predictable, the cost to the public, immense. Now Silberman is big on purpose, and I agree that lack of purpose, unwillingness to "think seriously and deeply about purpose", is a theme in our failure. But purposefulness has a history, too, and it is spotted. Zacharias was not without a sense of purpose. I don't think Silberman draws out the full importance of his own recounting of the history of reform. And he fails to temper his optimism with a realistic assessment of the complex political and economic historical processes inside of which reforms occur. The question we are left with is this: is Silberman's understanding of what he is about rich enough, his historical roots deep enough, to give one some confidence that the events he cites with optimism, as well as the enormous positive response to his own book, do not signal the beginning of another extravagant fad, this time called, with conspicuous capitals, Informal Education?

A Responsible Starting Point

Of course Silberman is not entirely responsible for the response his book gets. People in search of a fad will find one willy-nilly.

The book gives us something to build upon. There is much in addition to the broad themes I have touched. There is thoughful discussion of the rebellious temper of the times. There is the very fine effort to summarize the broad field of research and theory which bear upon the informal approach to schooling. There is an honest effort to deal with the special problems pertaining to schools attended predominantly by poor and non-white populations. There is a most useful synthesis of views of the kinds of damage bad schooling can do. There are cogent insights (his treatment of the *survival structure,* p. 151 ff.). There is a fairly continuous transcendence of the trivial and the inane. The problem is how to use what Silberman has given. If we take seriously the proposition that there is indeed a crisis of cataclysmic dimension, and if we recognize that crises are seldom successfully resolved by fads, and if we treat Silberman's vision with both respect and skepticism, and if we are willing to place Silberman's picture of the schools in the context of a broader analysis of failing social institutions, then we may find that *Crisis in the Classroom* can help us along to a responsible starting point. No mean accomplishment.

Note

1. Isaiah Berlin, *Four Essays on Liberty* (London: Oxford University Press, 1969).

IV

Comment on Charles E. Silberman's *Crisis in the Classroom*

Stuart Maclure

The strength of Silberman's approach is its readability and its thoroughness. Its weakness is that the remedy he proposes—the reincarnation of progressive education with a new English accent—amounts to an anti-climax when set against the devastating challenge which he has earlier laid down.

Silberman and his team have waded through an immense quantity of writing about education. With copious quotation and brilliant compression, he has served up an overview which, to the external observer at least, is impressive and illuminating. He has, moreover, started at the beginning by insisting on putting radical questions about the aims of education in the forefront and refusing to beg these by simply defining education (as most of us are obliged to do most of the time, life being short) as what happens in schools and colleges. In particular he expounds once again the sanity and penetration of Alfred North Whitehead and the liberalism of John Dewey and by so doing exposes the intellectual shallowness of most no-nonsense educational writing.

His insistence on a philosophical analysis of aims and purposes leads on logically to an appraisal of the present and the paradox of the American education—a world wide phenomenon in extreme form—which is that the more nearly it achieves the limited goals it serves, the more severely it is being criticised. While most of the indices (more university students, more Ph.D.s, more high school graduates, higher standards of achievement; less dropping out, more links between education perseverance and vocational suc-

cess) show continued and continuing movement towards full participation in a system of universal education, other signs seem to
indicate an educational system on the edge of disaster. At times the
system seems about to explode under the pressures of race, ethnicity, urban disadvantage, political strife and a crisis of values
which is beginning to add up to the cultural revolution of which
the prophets have long been preaching.

Having shown that the more nearly the system approaches fulfillment, the less willing Americans are to tolerate its inherent
weaknesses, Silberman goes on to describe and impale on the end
of his scavenger's stick, one by one, the education innovations of
the past 15 years. Unfairly, I think, he sets up first an aunt Sally.
Curriculum reform and technological innovation, he says, were
meant to bring about a revolution in the 10 years from 1955.
Using the excessive optimism of the early period as a stick with
which to beat the modest changes which have emerged at the end,
he concludes that this reform of curriculum and method has failed,
heaves a somewhat ostentatious sigh and sheds a weary tear. This
sounds, in the context, a bit like a parody of America's magnificent
moodiness, fluctuating between wild enthusiasm and the sad but
recurring discovery that miracles don't happen. It is rather like the
hopefulness of the man who always assumes that the sign "Under
New Management" is going to mean better service, and who has to
discover time and again that innovation is a neutral word.

In truth, of course, it is going to take much more than fifteen
years to see the consequences of the upsurge of educational innovation which began in the mid-fifties. The schools are still run, in the
main, by teachers and administrators who were trained before
many of the changes and new developments had had time to make
any impact. And surely the changed approach people are taking to
the curriculum should not be regarded as a once for all remaking
of the school program but as the initiation of new ways of looking
at curriculum, new ways of looking at schools, new ways of looking
at children and new ways of looking at the role of the teacher. This
is not a process which can—or should—work itself out in a few
years of intensive effort. If, as Silberman suggests, this is what people hoped for with some of the arrogance of external experts,
secure in their university observation posts, it was excessively
naive. More likely it had something to do with the overconfidence
which is encouraged by competition for funds and by the uplifting
North American assumption that problems are to be solved rather
than to be lived with.

At all events, Silberman has little difficulty in pointing out that
none of the current innovations is a panacea and that most of them
are no more than instruments, in that they seek better ways of
doing what is now done, rather than finding better things to do.

Readers in England will get some wry satisfaction from the devastating put-down of the earlier claims.

Computer Assisted Instruction

Anyone who had the experience of sitting in Robert Louis
Bright's office, when he was Associate Commissioner of Education
in charge of the Bureau of Research back in 1966, and heard him
unfolding his vision of the computer-assisted future must have had
the profoundest scepticism—especially when Mr. Bright made it
clear that in his brave new world the role of the teacher had still to
be worked out and that nobody knew enough about individual
learning processes to program a computer so that it could bring to
bear its potential sensitivity to the needs of each child.

Society and the Schools

Silberman uses this run down on current innovation to lead into
the second half of his book with a terse summary of what he has
discovered about the philosophical foundations and pedagogic
superstructure of American education. As everyone does sooner or
later, he comes back to the umbilical cord between society and the
schools. "Our most pressing educational problem . . ." he writes,
"is not how to increase the efficiency of the schools; it is how to
create and maintain a humane society. A society whose schools are
in-humane is not likely to be humane itself."(p. 203)

Here it is again, the mood of disenchantment and disillusion. A
cynic might observe that what Mr. Silberman has described at such
length is an educational system which only too faithfully reflects
the tensions of the society it serves. And not only is this what you
would expect, but you would be suspicious of and sceptical about
an educational system which tried to run counter to the confused
will of society and the arrogance of the master minds who sought
to direct it. All the talk about the need to clarify the aims of education and challenge the present easy assumptions is helpful only up
to a point. The critical fact about education is the confusion of
values in society at large and the need to educate people for
pluralism, conflict, and tension rather than impose upon them and
their schools a new vision summoned up from the present mess by
some supreme effort of good will.

With his feet on the ground, Silberman recognises these inherent
limitations. He is a reformer rather than a utopian, John Amos

Comenius not Jean-Jacques Rousseau. He culls some of the best of the radical insights of John Holt and Edgar Friedenberg and James Herndon and the rest of them while putting his finger on their implied upper class snobbery against lower-middle class teachers, and what he calls (not without a touch of snobbery of his own?) "the spiteful bigotry of many self-made intellectuals."(p. 141)

The problem remains, however; how can you clearly recognize that the schools are society's poodle with limited scope for independent action, yet at the same time construct a convincing program of reform in strictly educational terms? It is a dilemma which the genuine radicals avoid by regarding educational reform as a means of getting back at the society they hate. Silberman rejects the barrenness and circularity of the *student as nigger* ideology, which comes close to condemning improvements in education in case they should make the vicious system temporarily more tolerable. But while he explains and by implication attacks the role of education as an instrument of social control, it is not always clear whether he wants to devise some other, more acceptable method of bringing forward operating elites within society, or simply wants more social justice within the education system and, hence, more social mobility. It would demand another triumph of hope over experience to believe that more precisely fair techniques of using the educational system for social control would, by themselves, give much more satisfaction. As Silberman points out, a really efficient meritocracy would be hell. As for alternative criteria for advancement, most of those which come to mind like heredity, intimidation, bribery, crime, political or religious tests, have already been tried at different times and in different places and rejected because education seemed a fairer idea. Nothing has happened lately to make them look manifestly superior to the present mess.

The *Free* School

In the light of all this, Silberman's advocacy of the English primary school can only be seen as part of a search for a key to open up a wide range of locked doors. It would be unfair to accuse him of offering the *free* school as a panacea. But this certainly seems to be the main plank in his program, and even those who believe in the new English primary school would have doubts about its capacity to bear the weight which Silberman puts upon it. There can be no doubt about the deep impression which the progressive schools of Leicestershire, Oxfordshire and London (to name the principal areas on the visitors' circuit) have made on American observers. In some cases it seems almost akin to a conversion experience. Clearly Silberman and his team were profoundly moved by what they saw . . . but it is difficult even for a patriotic Englishman to resist the conclusion that he tended to see what he desperately needed to see. I have no doubt that the English schools visited which were committed to the full gospel of freedom and integrated studies have added enormously to the sum of human happiness. I don't dispute the relevance of this to the American scene. It is simply that Silberman's thoroughness did not force him to give much prominence to the serious questioning of the theoretical basis of the new primary school by men like Professor Robert Peters and Professor G.H. Bantock.

Silberman explains the new approach to primary schooling as the product of three intellectual sources. First of all there is a philosophy of education which goes back through Dewey to Johann Pestalozzi, Maria Montessori and, by inference, Rousseau. Second, there is a theory of intellectual and physical development which draws mainly on Jean Piaget. And thirdly there is the practical pedagogy of the primary school head teachers and their staffs, assisted and encouraged by the school inspectors, the HMIs (Her Majesty's Inspectors) and the staffs of advisers employed by the local education authorities.

In practice, as Silberman shows, this educational revolution has been teacher-controlled and teacher-mediated. By far the strongest element is the practical success which teachers have achieved, or seem to have achieved, by using informal methods. *Success* in this context means the achievement of a range of social objectives and the creation of a warm and happy atmosphere as well as the acquisition of basic skills. As Silberman stresses, this has not been done by imposition from on top (though it would be a mistake to underestimate the manipulative skills of some of the administrators, it is no coincidence that development has been most marked where the men at the top have been fully committed to the new way), but by setting the teachers free to experiment and gradually apply methods originally thought appropriate only for the nursery school, to older age groups. The colleges of education have played an important part in this (it had become the new orthodoxy in the colleges while still only being characteristic of a minority of schools), but it is a change which has genuinely emerged from experience, not from blinding revelation or administrative ukase. And it has emerged over a period of time. For seventy or eighty years optimistic commentators have consistently overestimated both its achievements and the extent to which it has prevailed.

As first and foremost a practical response to the day-to-day encounter of teachers and children, it is a good deal stronger in practice than in theory. The Piagetian psychology is hazily grasped by the average primary school teacher who is less likely to be influenced by the experiments of a Swiss experimental psychologist than by the rules of thumb which she has developed out of a few popularised precepts. At its best the result is good, most impressive to observe, and conducive to good relations and a happy atmosphere, with children learning well or better a wider range of skills than in a formal school. At its worst, it probably justifies the caricature of progressive education which middle aged secondary school teachers in England still like to believe in, where the children are engaged in an unordered round of miscellaneous activity at a level of superficiality which permits the lazy to go through school without learning and never being obliged to concentrate their minds on any purposeful activity.

It is not necessary to quote examples of this kind of criticism, which is usually laced with prejudice (like much of the favorable comment); the objectives of the new primary school are different from those of the old; no simple comparisons can be made because it is not possible to compare like with like. What is clear is that the new primary school still accepts the obligation to initiate all the children into the basic skills and that this demands a high degree of structure and teacher control if the teacher is going to be able to ensure, informally, that all the children participate fully in the educational experience. As Silberman points out, many of the most successful (and enthusiastic) exponents of the new primary education were trained and gained their first experience in formal schools. They have needed no convincing that it was as important for a child to learn to read and do arithmetic in an informal classroom as it was in a formal one. Their technique has been tested to the limit; in many cases but not all, they have been able to cope and keep a check on all their children's progress without resort to traditional methods. But they have been pragmatists, working out their own salvation as they went along, exploiting the enthusiasm which release from the tyranny of silence and stillness, chalk and talk, can engender, but never losing sight of the main objective. The question is still open as to how future generations to whom the new methods represent unquestioned orthodoxy, will make out.

More on the English Schools

Many of the factors which have produced the English primary school seem to be indigenous to post-war Britain. I don't think it is any coincidence that it has flowered at a time when England has lost a good deal of its aggressive cutting edge in commerce and diplomacy. It assumes that virtues of cooperation are superior to those of competition. It assumes that the enjoyment of the here and now is more important than subordination to future training. It rejects methods of teaching which depend on intimidation or the promise of future reward for the motivation of children. It places high importance on *useless* activity such as movement and art.

Not surprisingly its critics are to be found among the academic rigorists who have clear ideas about educational objectives, expressed strictly in terms of examination success and entrance qualifications into university or college. In many cases their criticism is laced with a genuine concern for social justice; they fear that children who have been deprived of the benefits of formal teaching in a narrow, predetermined curriculum will never catch up in the race, which begins in the secondary school, and that the children who need the discipline of formal teaching most are those with least social advantages.

It also runs directly contrary to the political philosophy of the Heath Government. Whereas it can be seen in retrospect as belonging to the post-war concensus which somehow linked Clement Attlee, Winston Churchill, Harold Macmillan and Harold Wilson in an unholy alliance, the modern primary school is anathema to everything that the new Tories stand for and not least to the philosophy of the Secretary of State for Education, Mrs. Margaret Thatcher.

This could well bring, in time, a backlash in England. The first signs of it can be seen in the so-called Black Papers, published by the *Critical Quarterly,* which attempted a concerted attack on progressive educational methods, mobilizing those concerned with basic education on the one hand, and those affronted by revolting students on the other. It would be remarkable if these quasi-political considerations are not still more to the fore in the United States where societal pressures on the education system are far stronger than in England, and where the independent role of the teacher is seen quite differently. In England, the new primary school is an expression of the primary school teacher's growing self-confidence. If imported from Europe and imposed as an administrative bright idea in the United States, it might still further undermine the teachers' confidence, as Silberman recognizes with his sensitive descriptions of the North Dakota New School and Professor Lillian Weber's work in New York.

The weakness of the English primary school and the Plowden Report which is the fullest expression of what it stands for, is just at the philosophical level which Silberman rightly places at the forefront of the discussion. The pedagogic insights of practical teachers will have to be discovered again by anyone who seeks to recreate it. Piaget's psychology will continue to exert an influence at the theoretical level. But the philosophical confusion ought not to be reimported into the United States. Too much of it is not more than a second-hand version of ideas which ran to seed in America in the thirties.

Professor Peters, the professor of educational philosophy at the London University Institute of Education, has pointed out(1) that the new primary school has inherited a series of confused ideas about child development. He points to a key paragraph in the Report at the end of Chapter 15. . . .

The school sets out deliberately to devise the right environment for children to allow them to be themselves and to develop in the way and at the pace appropriate to them. It tries to equalise opportunity and to compensate for handicaps. It lays special stress on individual discovery, on first-hand experience and on opportunities for creative work. It insists that knowledge does not fall into neatly separate compartments and that work and play are not opposite but complementary. A child brought up in such an atmosphere at all stages of his education has some hope of becoming a balanced and mature adult and of being able to live in, to contribute to, and to look critically at the society of which he forms a part.

This implies a great many dubious or misleading things about children and their *nature* and a theory of *development* which is not spelled out in detail but remains unsatisfactory throughout the report and illustrates the effort to be all things to all men. The emphasis on the child as the agent of his own learning is rooted in faith rather than any particular empirical investigation. It is another way of asserting the value of the individual over against the state; but as it stands in the Plowden philosophy, it implies an unconditional belief in the development of individual selves, without any value system which asserts that some kind of selves are better than others. Anyway, it is all inclined to be a high-falutin' way of saying little. As Peters puts it, "talk of development, like talk of children's *needs*, is too often a way of dressing up our value judgments in semi-scientific terms."

If, as Peters postulates (and as I read him, Silberman would agree) "education involves initiation into what is thought to be worthwhile", then the teacher must have a much more positive role to play than the "child-grower who manipulates the environment so that children will proceed from discovery when they are *ready*". Nor, unless you hold a *rucksack* or *rag bag* view of knowledge does the dismissal or ordered learning appear self-evident.

It is not that the outcome of the inadequate philosophy of most primary schools is necessarily bad, nor yet that anybody wants the school to revert to earlier and less liberal ways. It is simply that kind hearts will not indefinitely serve as substitutes for tough minds, and sooner or later teachers will have to fall back on their basic philosophical premises. As it is, those weaknesses in practice which are most obvious, happen to coincide with the philosophical weakness. For example, the horticultural theory of child development can let a child grow up from one experience to another without really learning anything. Similarly, the process of learning by discovery has obvious social merit in an open school with a proliferation of teaching material. But the theory of the discovery method is sketchy, indeed, as Professor Bantock and Professor Peters have both pointed out. And there is a real danger that teachers will leave their common sense behind and go overboard for the discovery method, not because they can see the benefits, but because they are buoyed up by a mistaken belief in its theoretical validity. Modern methods demand a high degree of structural design by the teacher, which does not follow logically from the educational theories on which they are based.

If the English primary school can travel and succeeds in putting down roots in America, it will take on its own form from its new surroundings, and visitors from Leicestershire will troop over, in their turn, to see the new species. But as I understand it, Silberman is arguing that the stimulus to change thus offered will extend throughout the system and this will depend on a wide range of other factors. What would be disastrous would be to import a new orthodoxy called *the English primary school.* If the English primary school is anything, it is an evolutionary phenomenon; an expression of professional freedom and the willingness to apply this in constantly changing circumstances to the education of young children and adolescents.

England would have a lot to answer for if it sent across the Atlantic a strait-jacket instead of a new pair of overalls.

Note

1. R. S. Peters (editor), *Perspectives on Plowden* (London: Routledge and Kegan Paul, 1969).

V

Changing the Schools: Proposals and Possibilities

David A. Goslin

For the past four years I have been engaged in a task very simi-lar to that undertaken by Charles Silberman; namely, to make some sense out of the vast array of proposals and propositions, criticisms and counter-criticisms, programs and prescriptions that have been advanced by those who feel, as I and Mr. Silberman do, that schools in America are badly in need of improvement. The number of such persons, both inside the educational profession and out, has grown rapidly during the last two decades, as has the number and variety of solutions to educational problems offered.

The problems themselves have been approached from many dif-ferent perspectives; each point of view generating a different set of priorities, a different proposal or set of proposals (each for radical reform), a new sense of urgency on the part of educators and the public alike. We were made conscious of the deficiencies of racially segregated schools and then of the difference between desegrega-tion and integration. Our hopes were raised by the promise of shortcuts to learning through programmed textbooks, computer as-sisted instruction, and educational television, only to discover that these techniques offered no instant panacea. Smaller classes and larger classes, homogeneous grouping and heterogeneous grouping, Head Start and second chance, decentralization and performance contracting, educational vouchers and community control, teacher aids and better teacher training have all had their advocates. The list could be extended with ease.

What is remarkable is that through it all the schools have

remained relatively unchanged, as has the basic process of education in America. The vast majority of children spend their days in classes that are not *significantly* different from those their parents and grandparents encountered a generation or two ago. To be sure, more children attend school for more years, schools and school systems have grown in size and, consequently, heterogeneity, new gadgets and new materials have been added, and support systems have become vastly more complex. But little evidence can be found of fundamental changes in the way teachers teach or how children learn or what they learn in most schools. If schools have not improved any, they have probably not gotten any worse, at least in absolute terms.

Why, then, all the ferment over education? One reason is that, like everything else in our society we *expect* improvement in our educational system. A second and more important reason is that as our society as a whole has changed, new social problems have generated new demands on our educational systems; for example, demands for a more equitable distribution of educational opportunities, for a larger supply of highly trained manpower, and for better preparation of young people for coping with a rapidly changing society and world. In relation to our needs, it is clear that our schools have increasingly been found wanting.

Crisis in the Classroom is a valiant attempt both to pinpoint present deficiencies of our schools and classrooms, and to suggest remedies for these deficiencies. I found myself agreeing with virtually everything that Mr. Silberman says. Although his basic argument can be seen as a simple reformulation of educational principles that have been widely advocated (and used, I suspect, by the best teachers and the best schools) for a long time, he has succeeded in bringing these principles to life in a way which represents a significant step forward for the field of education. In particular, the provision of a conceptual framework (in this case drawn from the work of Jean Piaget) from which practical steps may be derived is virtually unique in educational writing, although this is not the case among several social scientists who have concerned themselves with education, among others U. Bronfenbrenner (1), Morris Janowitz (2), David Goslin (3, 4), B. F. Skinner (5), O. K. Moore (6), a situation which has much to do with the botch that is made of many attempts to implement innovative ideas in real school settings.

Rather than extol the many virtues of Mr. Silberman's book, however, I should like to focus on what I perceive to be its shortcomings. In one sense, much of what follows cannot be construed as criticism of Mr. Silberman or of *Crisis in the Classroom,* since it is always unfair to attack an author for not writing the book you hoped he would write. On the other hand, potential effectiveness of the book Mr. Silberman *did* write is, in my view, reduced as a consequence of the things it fails to take into account.

Understanding the Learning Process

Mr. Silberman's central argument draws its support from three sources: 1) a careful (and extremely useful) reexamination of the philosophy and goals of education 2) the developmental theories of Jean Piaget, and 3) the example of their practical application in the informal classrooms of the new English primary schools. The articulation of these perspectives on the learning process makes a convincing case for the necessity of reexamining many of the practices widely employed in American elementary and secondary schools, as well as in the majority of British schools that may still be described as *traditional* or formally organized. In emphasizing the need for richer educational environments, greater freedom for pupils to develop at their own pace and in self-determined directions, and for substantially greater flexibility on the part of teachers (as well as administrators), Mr. Silberman is in the center of a growing body of educators. Both in America and abroad, educators have become aware of the stultifying effect of strict reliance on didactic teaching combined with highly structured classroom procedures and inflexible administrative organization of schools and school systems as a whole. While they are careful to distinguish between the new *informal education* and past unfortunate misinterpretations of *progressive* theories of education (which often resulted in total lack of structure and, in some cases, substance), they see the other extreme as equally, if not more, harmful.

Scientific support for these principles comes from a great variety of sources; including, in addition to Piaget, Jerome Bruner (7), Lawrence Kohlberg (8) and O. K. Moore (9). At the same time, however, Mr. Silberman fails to take into account a number of theorists and researchers whose work, while not necessarily contradictory to the view taken in *Crisis in the Classroom,* at the very least adds significant dimensions to our understanding of the learning process and to the implications of this understanding for educational practice.

First, Mr. Silberman avoids consideration of the substantial contributions made by behavior theorists ranging from the early work of C. L. Hull (10), B. F. Skinner (11) and others to the more recent studies of J. L. Gewirtz (12). The concept of operant conditioning, as developed by Skinner, for example, has had significant application to educational practice in the form of programmed textbooks, computer assisted instruction, and a variety of other widely used techniques. More important than the technological innovations that have resulted from their work is the fact that much learning can and does take place in accordance with principles enunciated by various formal learning theories, including reinforcement, and contiguity of stimulus and response.

Nor does Mr. Silberman concern himself with the growing body of research on processes of imitation, identification, and/or modeling which appear to be a crucial part of early as well as later learning. Irrespective of current wrangles over the extent to which imitative behavior is mediated by more basic processes, such as reinforcement or contiguity, the existence of the phenomenon raises important practical questions concerning the conditions under which the behavior of others, including teachers, will be imitated. The effect on children of exposure to different kinds of models (for example, on television), and the structuring of educational institutions should be studied so as to provide a sufficiently wide range of adult as well as peer influences on a child's behavior. U. Bronfenbrenner (13), for example, has suggested that a major cause of our educational problems is the practice of American schools to isolate children in age-graded groups, which prevent exposure to a wide range of potentially significant models, including adults outside the school as well as older and younger children within the school.

The latter view, of course, is fully compatible with Mr. Silberman's proposals for informal education. By itself, however, Piagetian theory does not lead one to the conclusion that exposure to a *wide variety* of adult models is a necessary component of humane and effective education. Nor does it lead one to pay close attention to the way in which rewards and punishments should be distributed in the classroom (an especially complex issue in a society that places great demands on schools to evaluate and maintain records of the performance of individual children as a basis for future educational and occupational opportunities). The design of optimally effective learning environments requires such attention to detail, based on a careful analysis of the best available research and theory in all areas, if we are to arrive at fully intelligible and widely *applicable* conceptions of what ought and ought not to go on in the classroom.

In this context, it is worth noting that Mr. Silberman himself falls into the trap of failing always to distinguish between innovations in the educational environment that are central to his theory and those that are not. Thus, for example, it is not inconceivable that some educators may put fresh flowers and live turtles in their classrooms, but fail to remember that informal learning also means

providing a variety of experiences *outside* the classroom as well as
in it.

The Social Context

It is almost unnecessary to point out that schools do not exist in
a social vaccum. What goes on in the school, the way it is organized, the attitudes held by children and teachers alike towards
it, and a host of other factors are affected by the social and cultural
environment in which the school is situated. Although Mr. Silberman acknowledges the importance of such influences at various
points throughout his book, his primary focus on the classroom
leads him away from a thorough analysis of their impact on the
learning process itself and on the problems of achieving educational reform in very different social settings. By drawing upon examples of informal education in a variety of English schools as
well as a few in this country ("ITEM: A classroom in a school in a
coal mining town in Yorkshire . . . .") (p. 250), he gives us the
impression that the necessary techniques are similar from one
school to the next and, more important, require only a willingness
to try on the part of teachers and administrators (an assumption I
will tackle more directly in the following section).

While I am optimist enough to agree that virtually anything is
possible in most settings, I do not conclude that characteristics of
families, peer group norms, communities, and governmental
agencies can be ignored if we are to achieve any substantial degree
of educational reform, nor can they be considered irrelevant even
to specific proposals for change. To take a trivial example,
enriching the learning environment is almost certain to require different kinds of materials in rural schools as opposed to urban ghetto schools if the interest of children is to be aroused initially and
maintained over time. Similarly, differential expectations of
children toward school, based on preexisting family and peer
group norms, must be handled in the light of a solid understanding
of these norms and expectations.

A major difference, it seems to me, between English schools and
an increasing number of American schools is the degree of authority over what goes on in the school that is accorded school officials
by parents and children alike. In community after community in
the United States parents are taking an increasingly active role in
attempting to influence, albeit with varying degrees of success,
school policies and practices. The widespread movement toward
decentralization in our large cities is symptomatic both of the dis-
gust with perceived bureaucratic inflexibility and a growing dis-

trust of the *experts*. Although promising in the sense that greater responsiveness to community needs and freedom from some constraints imposed by large scale bureaucracy may be achieved, more effective community control also carries with it the possibility that new, poorly understood, and therefore threatening, innovations may be blocked or substantially altered before they can be given a fair trial. Moreover, the increased vulnerability of administrators and teachers to parental criticism may have the effect of decreasing their willingness to take chances with new methods.

To a significant degree this has always been the case in America. Morris Janowitz (14) points out, for example, the oversimplification inherent in four widely held beliefs about large public school systems in this country; namely, 1) that there exists highly effective centralized authority; 2) that systems operate in a highly uniform and routinized way, 3) that teachers are over-professionalized, and 4) that there exists a lack of standards for performance. In fact, says Janowitz, many of the problems faced by our inner city schools result from a *lack* of effective centralized authority, the *inability* of this authority to change or even influence what actually goes on in schools, the *lack* of professional support for teachers, and the constraints imposed by *too much* reliance on formal standards for performance (for example, test scores)!

This analysis helps a great deal to explain why school systems in this country have not changed much, despite a longer period of harsh public and professional criticism than has been the case in England. The lack of consideration of organizational features of school systems along with characteristics of their social context leads to the final major deficiency in Mr. Silberman's book: his inability to come to grips directly with the problem of how to achieve reform.

Achieving Reform

Like many before him, Mr. Silberman clings to the optimistic view that demonstrating to a person the error of his ways and giving him a vision of something better will produce a change in his behavior. It is well known, however, that change, especially at the institutional level, requires a great deal more than desire and good will on the part of isolated individuals. By neglecting political and organizational features of our schools and school systems, along with the larger social context in which they are imbedded, Mr. Silberman fails at his ultimate task: to provide clear-cut means by which social theory can be translated into public policy.

The most important link in this chain involves the allocation of *responsibility*. Who must take responsibility for what aspects of the change process? What can and must be done to make it possible for individuals and organizations to take such responsibilities? What role is to be taken by teachers, principals, school superintendents, school boards, the P.T.A., teacher training institutions, state departments of education, and the Federal government? Clearly, all must be involved if widespread reform is to be achieved. But it is not enough to leave it at that; the initiatives, activities and responsibilities of each part of the system must be spelled out with full cognizance of existing constraints (as well as areas of latitude) on occupants of each position.

Consider, for example, the role of the teacher. Let us assume that all teachers, even within the most bureaucratic systems, enjoy, at a minimum, a few degrees of organizational freedom within which they can determine what procedures they will follow in their classrooms; degrees of freedom that, theoretically, would permit change in the direction of Mr. Silberman's ideal. Sheer demands on time and energy, however, may effectively prevent the exercise of such initiative, except in the case of the most highly dedicated and energetic. Possible solutions come easily to mind; greater involvement of teacher aids, an increase in the teacher force; cooperative arrangements among teachers, and so on. Each of these, however, requires initiative on the part of *other* participants in the system.

Resistance to change cannot be explained solely in organization terms, either. Mr. Silberman calls attention at the beginning of his book to the amount of inertia inherent in most complex systems, including the schools. Contributing to this inertia is a basic defense mechanism which is as common among educators as it is in other professions. I call it the "That's similar to what we are doing already" syndrome. It refers, simply, to the dissonance-reducing technique of finding aspects of one's current program that conform to the recommendations being made. The greater the anxiety generated, the greater will be the efforts made to reduce it.

Crisis in the Classroom, unfortunately, seems certain to produce a great deal of this sort of reaction on the part of educators. Not only is it anxiety arousing, but its heavy reliance on examples and its lack of a concise summary of the necessary conditions for establishing informal learning environments present serious problems in trying to decide what actually to do in the classroom.

Finally, Mr. Silberman does not deal, except in passing, with several major current attempts to stimulate educational reform on a broad scale. No mention is made, for example, of the educational voucher plan, which holds promise for helping to break down institutional barriers against change. Nor, astonishingly, does he acknowledge the existence and potential impact of the many Montessori schools throughout America (a movement which might have provided him with a more convenient and readily applicable model of informal education than that of the new English primary school although most Montessori schools concentrate on preschool education). The potential role of educational research, the emerging model schools program financed by the Federal government and the increasing involvement of commercial enterprise in education receive little, if any, attention.

Yet all are factors to be considered in the development of a model for change in American education. By focusing on certain aspects of the system, Mr. Silberman has added immeasurably to the depth of our vision of what education might become. This, at the very least, is a major step.

Notes

1. U. Bronfenbrenner, *Two Worlds of Childhood: U.S. and U.S.S.R.* (New York: Russell Sage Foundation, 1970).
2. M. Janowitz, *Institution Building in Urban Education* (New York: Russell Sage Foundation, 1969).
3. D. A. Goslin, *The School in Contemporary Society* (Glenview, Ill.: Scott, Foresman and Company, 1965).
4. _____, "The School in a Changing Society," *American Journal of Orthopsychiatry*, October, 1967, vol. 37, no. 5: 843-58.
5. B. F. Skinner, "The Science of Learning and the Art of Teaching", *Harvard Educational Review*, 1954, 24, 86-97.
6. O. K. Moore and A. R. Anderson, "Some Principles for the Design of Clarifying Educational Environments," in D. A. Goslin (Ed.), *Handbook of Socialization Theory and Research* (Chicago: Rand McNally and Company, 1969), chap. 10, 571-613.
7. J. S. Bruner, *The Process of Education* (Cambridge, Mass.: Harvard University Press, 1961).
8. L. Kohlberg, "Stage and Sequence: The Cognitive-Developmental Approach to Socialization," in D. A. Goslin (Ed.), *Handbook of Socialization Theory and Research*, chap. 6, 347-480.
9. Moore and Anderson, "Some Principles for the Design of Clarifying Educational Environments."
10. C. L. Hull, *Principles of Behavior* (New York: Appleton-Century, 1943).
11. B. F. Skinner, *The Behavior of Organisms* (New York: Appleton-Century, 1938).
12. J. L. Gewirtz, "Mechanisms of Social Learning: Some Roles of Stimulation and Behavior in Early Human Development," in D. A. Goslin (Ed.), *Handbook of Socialization Theory and Research*, chap. 2, 57-212.
13. Bronfenbrenner, *Two Worlds of Childhood.*
14. Janowitz, *Institution Building.*

VI

The Crisis of Purpose
and
Crisis in the Classroom

Mark R. Shedd
and Terry Borton

Charles Silberman's book, *Crisis in the Classroom,* is not about crisis in the classroom. Rather, as Silberman explains in his introduction, "This book is about educational purpose."(p. 10) What emerges from this dichotomy of title and stated subject is in fact a third entity: a comprehensive and persuasive argument for *informal education*. This argument has already received enthusiastic reviews and has stirred a remarkable series of action proposals. We are glad to add our tribute to the rest. But there *is* a crisis in the classroom, though Silberman concentrates on the everyday grimness of school reality. And there *is* a crisis of educational purpose, though Silberman barely touches the subject. We believe the two are related, and have found Silberman's book a provocative catalyst in defining for ourselves some important elements in that relationship.

Crisis in the Classroom hardly mentions the immediate crises that we and many other educators face daily: a yearly battle for funds to keep from closing the schools; a bloody clash between 4000 black students and the city police; sixteen simultaneous racial attacks at one high school; a teachers' strike so bitter that striking teachers would no longer talk to those who came in to teach the kids; forty-seven boys killed in gang warfare in our city last year; thirteen-year-old kids dying of drugs. These crises, which are front page news, are as disturbing as they are visible—at least as disturbing as the evidence that Silberman amasses to support his charge that "schools are the kind of institution one cannot really dislike until one gets to know them well."(p. 10)

We concur with Silberman that schools are "grim, joyless . . . oppressive and petty."(p. 10) We agree that some of this atmosphere stems from "mindlessness—the failure or refusal to think seriously about educational purpose."(p. 11) But no one who faces crises daily can believe, as Silberman does, that "mindlessness is the central problem."(p. 11) For situations do not reach the crisis stage unless someone *minds* what is happening, unless systems of meaning are threatened, unless purposes are in conflict.(1) We do not believe that school administrators, teachers, students, parents, teacher-trainers, and the larger community are mindless. We hear many mindful, purposeful voices clamoring to make a difference in the schools. Silberman's call for informal education is one such voice. Others, of every persuasion, can be heard at Board meetings or read in the Letters to the Editor of any city paper. There are many minds, many purposes—arguing, demanding, competing, seeking.

We believe that the most useful response to this struggle between different purposes lies not so much in proposing a single right answer—informal education or any other—as in finding the processes which will allow the crisis of purpose to be a means for growth.

Attaining a Purpose

Silberman explicitly states that he does not intend to write "an exercise in academic philosophy,"(p. 9) and indeed, much of the persuasiveness of his book arises from the way he discusses purpose through concrete examples. But the lack of a systematic philosophical approach makes it very difficult to determine to what degree the concrete examples actually recall purposes stated elsewhere. By combing through the book and abstracting those statements which explicitly define purpose, it is possible to bring together an overall paraphrase of Silberman's concept of education, which can then be compared with the actual programs he discusses:

Education must involve a fusion of thought, feeling, and action, (p. xii) a blend of cognitive and affective knowing, (p. 8) which leads to a moral life. (p. 9) Schools should be organized to facilitate joy in learning and aesthetic expression, to develop character, (p. 10) and to teach intellectual skills and academic knowledge, (p. 62) Schools should prepare students to work in the present and the future; to live a creative, humane, and sensitive life, to be able to educate themselves, experience beauty, and apply knowledge to life. (p. 114-115) Schools should allow a student to live fully and naturally as a child, (p. 116) while helping him develop the knowledge and skills he needs to make sense out of his experience—with himself, with others, and with the world. (p. 336)

This is a very impressive statement, but impressive statements of educational purpose are legion. Usually they are never attained because the lofty goals are overwhelmed by a combination of grinding trivia and jarring crisis. Only the most consistent operational procedures will turn statements of purpose into descriptions of program. We believe that successful goal attainment is directly related to how explicitly the goal is reflected in the means, or the actual practice. For instance, informal education very explicitly develops a balance between freedom and structure which clearly fulfills the goal of allowing a student to live fully and naturally as a child, while helping him develop the knowledge and skills he needs.

The statement of purpose is backed with hundreds of detailed examples of how it might be achieved. This well-substantiated balance between student and subject, freedom and structure, is the great contribution of informal education to schools, and the aspect of it which both its philosophers and its practitioners are most clear about. As a result, the balance gets learned. Children, (including some of our own kids) understand very clearly the purpose of the balance between freedom and structure which they experience. When asked why the class is set up as it is, they will state Silberman's goal, but in their own words: "It's so we can do what we want and still be learning stuff." These students are quite conscious of what is happening to them, and what it is for. They not only know; they know that they know.

But there are other purposes which are not as explicitly reflected by what happens in the classroom, and hence it is doubtful that a student learns them as well, or can articulate them so clearly. For instance, there is little or no explicit teaching in the affective domain, either in Silberman's book, or in most of the informal education classes we have visited. It is assumed that the goals of a "humane and sensitive life" and "a student's ability to make sense out of his experience with himself " will emerge out of the totality of what is happening in the classroom. There is rarely an explicit set of methods, or materials, or strategies, which will help students deal with the complexities of personal and inter-personal relations, value conflicts, or emotional growth. The crisis of human relations all around us in our classrooms and society indicates clearly that our children will not learn what they need to know by simply participating in the life around them, even in an informal class. Indeed, these crises, particularly as they arise in schools, argue for the desperate need to get a better, clearer, more conscious understanding of affective factors. These can then be taught explicitly, and integrated with the rest of learning in the same clear but wholistic way that informal education has already integrated the balance between structure and freedom.

Such programs exist, and can be a resource for exploring the potential of these methods, just as the programs Silberman cites help explain informal education. In Philadelphia, the Affective Education Development Program has devised a wide variety of courses, methods, and materials which combine explicit attention to affective processes and to subject content. (Some of these will be discussed in detail later.) In San Diego, the Human Development Training Institute has trained teachers in the use of a developmental program of affective education for elementary students.(2) In Santa Barbara, a Ford Foundation supported project has for several years been experimenting with the use of gestalt awareness training in the classroom, as well as incorporating other affective experiences drawn from the Esalen Institute.(3) In Amherst, Massachusetts, courses are being developed in "Education of the Self." (4) And *The Big Rock Candy Mountain*, a catalog of educational materials and strategies patterned on *The Whole Earth Catalog*, carries references to hundreds of other resources. (5)

The argument for explicit operational practices tied to goals in the affective domain applies equally well to those goals which deal with process knowledge: Schools should prepare students to work (in the present and the future); "to develop the knowledge and skills they need to make sense out of their experience . . ."(p. 336) Most informal education programs work at these goals through the media of traditional subject content. These subjects are usually taught in a way which emphasizes the process approach —learning "ways of doing" and applying that knowledge. But if students are expected to learn a more generalized process knowledge, then it also makes sense to teach them these processes in a more generalized form, rather than assume that transfer from specific content to general problem will automatically take place.

Again, there are programs which have been developed to teach students general process skills which can be applied in a conscious way to a wide range of subject matter, to a student's own personal life, and to the unknowns of the future. *The Productive Thinking Program* is a course in general problem-solving strategies for young children, using mystery stories in a cartoon format.(6) *Tools for Change* is a somewhat similar course, developed with the support of the Carnegie Corporation, and using games and puzzles as the media for teaching processes drawn largely from the information processing and computer fields.(7)

A much more explicitly computer-oriented program is being developed at the Massachusetts Institute of Technology's Artificial Intelligence Laboratory, using a simple computer-programming language so that young students can learn the problem solving processes basic to computers.(8) *Education for Student Concerns*, developed by the Philadelphia Affective Education Development Program, teaches explicit processes for learning more effectively in the personal and social areas, and uses a wide range of subject matter and media.(9) Such programs suggest that it is possible to create educational environments which will very explicitly fulfill Silberman's goals in both the affective and the process skills areas.

Developing
Educational Purposes

Even if Silberman's statements of purpose are backed with other operational procedures which are more likely to make them achievable, the question remains: Why these purposes? Compare them, for instance, with other current statements also backed with practice. "What Will You Be When You Grow Up?", a radical's beginning reader, concludes, "All the people should learn to read the books of the revolution and explain these books to other people . . . and learn to fight."(10) Young Muad' Dib, the hero of a futuristic underground best seller, *Dune,* learns how to maintain power by combining his mother's training in Bene Gesserit mind control with his father's action axiom, "Look for the feint within the feint within the feint."(11) And a Richard Brautigan poem advocates that free schools give "A + for Marcia's long golden beauty."(12)

The point is that people have very different notions of what life is all about, very different notions of how to live it, very different notions of how to prepare for it—in sum, very different purposes. The struggle of various individuals and groups—blacks, students, teachers, radicals, and conservatives—is what the crisis of purpose in the schools is all about. We do not believe that any single educational program—informal education or any other—will fulfill such diverse purposes. Certainly we do not believe that informal education should be forced down the throats of those who want a more structured approach. We believe that the struggle between different purposes is an important and necessary ingredient of education. It is the essence of the evolutionary process—that *competition in the market*—through which men can continue to adapt to the changing conditions of their lives. It is through such conflicts that new and different purposes come into focus. Unfortunately, these conflicts have often led to a narrowing and isolating of different purposes—retrenchment, bitterness, hostility. But conflicts also contain the possibility for reaching a better understanding of others' purposes, of the reasons they hold them, of the common ground to build on together.

The possibility is there, though at this point in man's development, it seems a fairly slight possibility. Men do not yet know enough about their own behavior to make their clashes of purpose lead to a growing understanding of common human needs. But the beginning of such an understanding may be emerging. Two of the most promising sources for man's increased self-understanding are the theoretical backgrounds for the two fields we discussed in some detail earlier—affective and process education. As Willis Harmon, Director of the Educational Policy Research Center at Stanford Research Institute, has suggested, (13) the "new Copernican revolution" of our time may be the shift of man's systematic *scientific* thought from the external world, to the inner world of human behavior and feeling. Similarly, the *information revolution* has shifted attention from bits of content, to the processes for handling them. Both of these developments have a particularly important bearing on a discussion of educational purpose. For man's affect is closely tied to his purposes, his meanings, his sense of what is and ought to be. And a process is in fact defined as a *purposive behavior*—one which has a sequence, and a method or an implied goal.

For several years, The Affective Education Development Program of the Philadelphia Public Schools has been trying to develop educational methods which combine both an explicit attention to affect, and an explicit attention to the processes through which people learn to sense what is happening to them, transform it into meaning, and then act upon it. The central method that has evolved from the Program's work is the use of feedback. Feedback is defined as information which allows a person to discriminate between his intended purpose, and what he actually achieves, so that he can correct his actions in order to achieve his purpose. Such feedback is the basis of consciousness itself, the central tool through which man can improve his effectiveness, and further evolve his own purposes.(14) The Affective Education Development Program has developed a number of methods for increasing consciousness, and hence, helping students discover what their own purposes are, and act effectively on them.

In the Classroom

Within the classroom context, the Affective Education Development Program transforms the concept of feedback into three basic questions which constitute the background structure for all Program curricula and methods. Using colloquial language which is easily comprehended by the students, these three questions are phrased as: *What's happening?* (What's happening here? What is actually going on?); *So What?* (How does what is happening relate to my purposes or intentions?); *Now What?* (On the basis of a comparison of what is actually happening and what my purposes are, do I now want to change my behavior?) Within the area covered by each of these questions, the Program has evolved or borrowed a large number of teaching strategies. A few examples will give a sense of how these methods can be used to respond to classroom crises, essentially by teaching students the processes which will allow them to cope more effectively with their affective concerns.

"What's Happening?"   The question, *What's Happening?* is extremely difficult to answer without the perspective of contrasting a given situation with something else. Hence, conflicting purposes of people in schools are difficult to see because the school has imposed a single idea of *What's Happening?* on all who participate in it. And one of the great advantages of the informal education which Silberman expounds is that it allows many students to do many different things and find many different answers to the *What's Happening?* question. Thus it becomes easier for a student to see whether or not he is productive if he can compare his own action with that of another student working on the same problem with a different approach. Informal education, in other words, provides the freedom which gives a student alternatives, and allows him to come up with different answers to the question. But it does not provide any help in generating those alternatives.

There are explicit processes which can be used to help students generate new alternatives for themselves and create the perspective from which to answer the question. For instance, in a large integrated high school, the racial tension erupted in an explosion of sixteen simultaneous beatings. Battle lines were drawn, white against black, with very little room for compromise. One Program teacher brought together students from both sides and asked them to reflect on *What's Happening?* They described the situation as it was—two polarized camps. Then she suggested that since there seemed to be no common ground, it was an appropriate time to try the process of brainstorming to see what possible common needs there could be. The students were taught the process—a procedure for generating new alternatives by getting down on paper all possible solutions to a problem, no matter how bizarre or silly, and not allowing anyone to censure any idea until all ideas are stated. When the exercise was over, they had a long list of common needs. Many, as required by the nature of the exercise, were silly or inconsequential common needs—clean socks, arms and legs. But others were of considerable more substance—need for safety in the school, need for good teachers, need to keep outside gangs away from school. The common ground was substantial enough so that they were willing to set aside their differences for awhile, and work together on ways to try to meet their shared needs.

There are a variety of other processes besides brainstorming which can be used to generate alternatives that give a perspective on *What's Happening?*. Consciously assuming a new point of view is one. Another is creating a matrix with a variety of categories which must be filled in. A complex and sophisticated one is *synectics,* (15) a process originally developed to help engineers and inventors be more creative, and now being applied in curricular approaches. The basic assumption of the synectics process is that creativity is metaphoric, and moves by associative links. Students are asked to find a metaphor for the problem which forces them to "make the familiar strange, and the strange familiar." The metaphors which emerge are then analyzed and used to give a new perspective on the problem, to encourage students to get outside the usual boxes of their thinking, and to create their own new options.

So What?   Once alternatives are established, it is important for students to clarify the implications and consequences of the purpose they are pursuing, the *So Whats?*. One method, of course, is simply to let the consequences happen as they may, hoping that the student will learn from experience. But experience is a harsh teacher. There are a number of ways of simulating experience closely enough to obtain the necessary information without getting badly burned. Role-playing (16) is one of the most effective of these simulation techniques because it can re-create so many elements of a situation. The use of fantasy and imagination (17) and simulation games (18) are two other ways of explicitly using man's ability to consciously work out the consequences of his actions without actually performing them.

Another way of clarifying purposes is to use the many points of view that exist in any class as a way of giving the teacher or a student personal *feedback* about his behavior.

Now What?   The *Now What?* question used by the Affective Education Development Program's curricula seems to suggest two basic processes when applied to crisis situations. If the various participants in the crisis understand *What's Happening* and the *So What's*, then they are ready either to negotiate between opposing purposes, or to cooperate on joint ones. Negotiation is essentially a way in which those who perceive themselves as adversaries can accommodate to each other's needs. Cooperation is the process in which those who perceive themselves as working toward the same goal can work together most effectively.

Explicit processes of negotiation have become more and more important in the Affective Development Program as its classes have moved toward an informal structure. One transitional step, though hardly of a crisis nature, developed when a teacher asked students to respond to a question and got two different answers. Rather than follow the usual procedure and pick up the answer which seemed most provocative, the teacher asked the two students to negotiate between them and see if they could reach an answer which both could accept. Discussion between the two was lively, with the rest of the class rooting for one or the other. At the end of a five minute period the two students had clarified their misunderstandings, and had reached agreement on an answer which was different than either of them had proposed in the beginning. This method has been further developed into a way of teaching physics by Cary Sneider, (19) who has students negotiate about the laws of physics which they propose to explain the phenomena they observe in their experiments.

With younger students the Program has begun to experiment with ways in which students can be allowed to *negotiate* their disagreements with adult *mediation* or supervision, but without interference. The usual procedure when two elementary students get into a fight is for the teacher to stop the fight and send them both to the principal. Recently, however, the Program acquired some *boffers*—long foam swords which are very light and flexible, and which come with the accoutrements of goggles, ear protectors, and gauntlets.(20) Using these boffers, students can battle each other with all of their strength, and yet not hurt each other. The Affective Program hopes that its initial experiments with boffers and other ways of helping students negotiate their disputes may be a beginning toward reducing the crisis of violence in our cities.

The process of cooperation is also one which students need to know in an explicit fashion, and which does not come easily or naturally, as anyone who has ever worked on a committee well knows. The Program has found it particularly difficult to establish cooperative groups which are not authoritarian, and do not have an appointed leader. One method which appears to be effective is to create a *learning group*—a group whose members are explicitly taught some of the basic processes of cooperation. One Program class is using such a group, likening it to a ship without a captain

—a self-sustaining and cooperative effort. The central figure is the navigator who provides information about where the ship is, where it is going, and how it intends to get there. Neither captain nor leader, he does not tell the group what to do, but reflects back to them what they are doing, and through such feedback keeps them conscious of their actions as a group. The teacher acts in an advisory role, coaching the navigator as the group tries to steer itself and accomplish its task. After such a coaching period, the class is broken into learning groups, which are sent off to develop their own tasks with major responsibility for carrying them out.

The System-wide Level

When we turn from the classroom, which in itself is a complex setting, to a system-wide level, where there are literally thousands of interacting forces, then the application of the *What, So What, Now What* sequence becomes much more difficult to establish. Nonetheless, we believe that making the various elements of the system conscious of their own purposes, able to understand the consequences of these purposes, and able to negotiate and cooperate, is the central problem facing a school system. During a period of rapid change, such as the one we are now experiencing, values and purposes cannot help but be in conflict. And unless a school system develops ways for those conflicts to be resolved, that system cannot survive.

What's Happening?   Over the last five years, we have tried a variety of methods to keep people aware of what is occuring in the school system. School Board meetings are now televised, live, in their entirety, and are considered the best show on the air by large audiences throughout the city. Within the school system itself, information about what is happening has been greatly expanded by substituting for the traditional newsletter a much more comprehensive house organ. Project Information Exchange also brings together ideas and resources from around the system and presents these in catalog form to all teachers. In addition, PIE operated a *finder's service* which will locate information on any subject within twenty-four hours.

Like students in a classroom, school administrators have little chance to understand *what's happening* in their own schools unless they can see it in some perspective provided by others' experience. Therefore, Philadelphia has incorporated dozens of experimental projects into the system and is placing principals in working positions within these experiments so that they can experience what it would mean for them to behave differently in their own home school.

Even with such facilities for information exchange, often it is only the crisis event which telegraphs the most significant information about *what's happening.* When four hundred policemen charged a group of protestors outside the administration building and a riot ensued, the resulting series of charges, newspaper headlines, and television specials focused attention on two key system questions which have been continually discussed in the following four years: Will the administration listen to and respond to the students? How will disruptive behavior be handled? Crisis in the system, like crisis in the classroom often dramatizes what is happening now and defines expectations of the future.

So What? The *So What?* question, the question for examining the intention and working out the possible consequences of an action, can be approached in two basic ways at a system-wide level. The first is by establishing clear procedures so that everyone in the system understands both the various processes for acting within the system, and the consequences of acting outside established procedures. One of the major accomplishments of the Philadelphia School Board has been the establishment of a Student Bill of Rights and Responsibilities which clearly spells out rights and responsibilities and defines procedures for working out grievances. Thus it is possible for a student to take action without having to create a crisis in order to get something done.

The second way in which systems can respond to the *So What?* question is by shortening the length of the feedback loop, thus making it possible for everyone in the system to find out what is happening, compare it with what was intended to happen, and correct the difference before the crisis stage. In Philadelphia, this has meant a major effort at decentralization, beginning first with the transfer of supportive services from the central administration into the district superintendent's offices. Proposals are being discussed which would decentralize the Board's powers into a variety of options which can be assumed by people within the eight districts. School-community coordinators, local people assigned to each school to act as a liaison between the principal and the community, also ensure quick communication and avoid the kind of misunderstanding which so often leads to clashes.

Now What? As at the classroom level, negotiating and cooperating are very effective processes at the system-wide level. Teachers unions are now well accepted and we have come to believe that, on the whole, such grouping together for the purpose of negotiating is a good thing for a system.

There are times, and this particular time is one of them, at which it is difficult to believe that such adversary negotiations will ever evolve into cooperation. At the minute, at least within this system, there is very little cooperation between anybody. Yet we see indications that some things spur the evolution of cooperation. Many of the steps we have discussed earlier help people feel that their needs are being met, and that there is a way for their concerns to be expressed, so that they become more willing to consider the needs of others. Negotiation in good faith, if continued long enough, can reach the point where the good faith is strong enough to develop cooperation. But negotiation by itself is not enough. Love, trust, happiness, excitement, tenderness, aspiration—these qualities which are most precious about human beings require the willing cooperation of freely-giving people.

Discipline, too, is a function of cooperation, and, in Philadelphia, it has unfortunately fallen between the cracks of the negotiating table.

Discipline is a job which no one wants. In negotiations it is passed from side to side, and eventually shunted off to a specialized few *disciplinarians*. These people become a force with no connection to the students or the teachers or the common educational exchanges which join them. The schools find themselves patrolled by policemen or quasi-policemen who do not know the students by name, and for whom every meeting is a confrontation, and all relations are on the basis of power, not person.

It is becoming clearer and clearer that without cooperation there will be no discipline, and the schools will be a chaos where terror and brute strength will rule, and guerrilla warfare will subvert. We do not know how cooperation can be achieved. What we do know is that it must. And we suspect that it is the consequences of trying to operate a system without cooperation that will force its development. Like those black and white students who brainstormed to find their common ground, students, teachers and administrators will find that their common ground is wide indeed—that it is as wide as the universal desire for learning and education, and that working together for those purposes can regenerate the love, trust, happiness, excitement, tenderness and aspiration which should characterize schools.

Crisis in
the School System

There *is* a crisis in the classroom. There is a crisis in the school system as well. Crisis has developed within these social structures because there is a crisis in the hearts and minds of individual human beings. It is a crisis of purpose, a search for new meaning in a new time. In part, this search can be met by providing the informal education which Silberman so exhaustively describes. But only in part. The conditions of "grim, joyless, oppressive, and petty" tedium on which Silberman builds so much of his case for informal education have existed in schools for half a century and more. Most of us are the products of such a system. Continuing crisis, however, is a new development, and cannot be met by simply changing a formal education to an informal one. We are not sure that it can be met through the procedures we have described here, for the crises are mounting, one upon another, faster than we can respond. We know that, like everyone else, we are barely holding our own. However, if the crisis is defined as one of purpose— as one of the heart and of the mind—then at least we know to work explicitly with the emotions of the heart and the thought processes of the mind. We can begin asking the questions which will help people use their human powers of consciousness in order to fulfill their own purposes, in harmony with the purposes of others.

Notes

1. Silberman is sometimes ambivalent on this point. His main charge is that "mindlessness is the central problem" (p.11), but later he says that "the crisis is real, involving as it does the most basic questions of meaning and purpose—the meaning and purpose of life itself." (p.28). We agree with the later diagnosis. It is the competing answers to basic questions that create crisis, not the mindless apathy of those who do not question.
2. Harold Bessel and Uvalo Palomares, *Methods in Human Development* (San Diego, Calif.: Human Development Training Institute, 1967).
3. George Brown, *Human Teaching for Human Learning* (New York: Viking Press, 1971).
4. Gerald Weinstein and Mario Fantini, *Toward Humanistic Education: A Curriculum of Affect* (New York: Praeger Publishers, 1970).
5. Sam Yanes, *Big Rock Candy Mountain* (Menlo Park, Calif.: Portola Institute, 1971).
6. Martin Covington, et al., *The Productive Thinking Program* (Berkeley, California: Education Innovation, Inc., 1967).
7. David Straus, et al., *Tools for Change* (Berkeley, Calif.: Interaction Associates, Inc., 1969).
8. Artificial Intelligence Laboratory, Massachusetts Institute of Technology, Cambridge, Mass. Attn. Dr. Seymour Papert.
9. Terry Borton and Norman Newberg, *Education for Student Concerns* (Philadelphia, Pa.: Philadelphia Board of Education, 1968). For a more complete description of these general process courses, see Terry Borton, "What's Left When School's Forgotten," *Saturday Review*, April 18, 1970.
10. *This Magazine is about Schools,* Fall, 1970.
11. Frank Herbert, *Dune* (New York: Ace Books, 1965).
12. Robert Greenway and Sally Rasberry, *Exercises* (Freestone, Calif.: Freestone Publishing Co., 1971).
13. Willis Harmon, "The New Copernican Revolution," in *The Big Rock Candy Mountain Supplement* (Menlo Park, Calif.: Portola Institute, Fall, 1970).
14. Terry Borton, *Reach, Touch and Teach: Student Concerns and Process Education* (New York: McGraw Hill, 1970), gives a general introduction to this approach. A more theoretical examination of the assumptions by

the same author is contained in "Private Experience and Public Knowledge" (Cambridge, Mass.: Unpublished thesis, Harvard Graduate School of Education, 1970).

15. William Gordon, *The Metaphorical Way of Learning and Knowing* (Cambridge, Mass.: Synectics Education Systems, 1968).

16. Mark Chesler and Robert Fox, *Role-Playing Methods in the Classroom* (Chicago: Science Research Associates, Inc., 1966).

17. Richard Jones, *Fantasy and Feeling in Education* (New York: New York University Press, 1968).

18. Richard Zieler, *Games for School Use* (Yorktown Heights, N. Y.: Center for Educational Services and Research, 1969).

19. Cary Sneider, "A Laboratory and Discussion Approach to High School Science Teaching," *The Physics Teacher,* January, 1971.

20. "Boffers" are available from the Boffing Institoot, 190 Emmet Court, San Francisco, Calif.

VII

Fantasies in a
Place Called "School"

William C. Kvaraceus

In the Foreword to August Aichorn's classic *Wayward Youth,* Freud indicated that in his youth he ". . . accepted it as a byword that the three impossible professions are teaching, healing, and governing . . ." Silberman's *Crisis in the Classroom* tends to reconfirm, like a pile driver, that teaching is still an impossible profession.

In his thoughtful and painstaking work, Silberman presents an anatomy of the American educational system. His analysis has been preceded by a long chain of critical studies that have attempted to point up the deficiencies in the educational system, how schools should be changed, and how teacher education could be improved. Among the earlier critics the following could be included: Jacques Barzun, Albert Lynd, Robert M. Hutchins, Arthur Bestor, James B. Conant, Paul Goodman, James Koerner, John Holt, Peter Schrag, Herbert Kohl, and Jonathan Kozol. Like Silberman's *Crisis in the Classroom,* all their volumes enjoyed wide circulation among the general public and within the professional community. But Silberman's volume will easily lead this list as the "best seller". He has succeeded in getting the professional educators and teachers to listen and to accept his findings and major recommendations, without any questioning of his motives, his data, or his conclusions. The Educational Establishments are taking Silberman—book, line, and sinker.

What explains the calm and rational reading of this text by the teaching community? The earlier volumes, almost without exception, left the educators up tight, angry, and defensive. They felt under personal attack as though their intellectual integrity and professional status were being questioned—and questioned with brutal third degree methods. The result was widespread panic in the educators' camps. Sidney Hook, a distinguished professor of philosophy from New York University, speaking at a meeting of the American Association of Colleges for Teacher Education in Chicago in 1954, undertook to answer Lynd, Bestor, and Hutchins. Paul E. Elicker, executive secretary of the National Association of Secondary School Principals, responded in the June 11, 1954, issue of *Collier's* to the question "How Good Are Our Schools?" in an obvious and thin whitewash over what and how the children were being taught.

Unlike his predecessors, Silberman is never snide, sneering, or contemptuous of teachers and their trainers. He is consistently understanding, sympathetic, and scholarly. In fact he commiserates with them openly and sees them as persons "who work hard and long at one of the most difficult and exacting jobs, but who are defeated by institutions which victimize them no less than their students." (p. x) Through his whole hearted empathy for teachers and his deep concern for the school and the child, he establishes strong rapport with his reader even before he gets into the first chapter.

Silberman surrounded himself with a most distinguished company of advisors who assisted him throughout his "nearly four years of intensive study, travel, research, and writing about teaching and learning." (p. ix)

Finally, if Silberman needed any more credibility, the fact that his three year study was commissioned by the Carnegie Corporation should leave no doubts in the reader's mind. Among his critic-predecessors, only Conant enjoyed similar backing. Silberman has no axe to grind, while the earlier commentators appeared to wage a personal vendetta against teachers and their trainers, jabbing away with their own brand of education.

Common Classroom Fantasies

As Silberman discloses the grim realities in his careful anatomy of the classroom, he painfully punctures a large number of fantasies that have been shared by school people, particularly those who work at the *higher levels* including administrators, supervisory and curriculum personnel, guidance workers, psychologists, and, of course, professors of education and educational researchers. Obviously these individuals do not come in daily contact with large numbers of children who inhabit classrooms. Since the trainers and supervisors are more apt to work with the IBM cards and not pupils, their perceptions of classroom reality will not be the same as those of the teacher who copes with problems of instruction and learning.

Fantasy:
The Schools Exist for the Pupil

Ostensibly, schools have been established for the benefit of the students. But Silberman indicates that schools serve their clients poorly and often treat them as something less than human. A major reason for the conditions outlined by Silberman can be found in the fact that schools also serve the needs of adults and other community agencies—public and private. When the needs of adults supercede the needs of pupils, it is the learners who are shortchanged. Thus, in the capitalistic tradition, the schools, like factories, try to produce more with the least investment, thus insuring the greatest saving and profit. In this sense, schools are Big Business and teaching is a common way to earn a living, often with a second job on the side. The result is that teachers perform like job-oriented technicians rather than pupil-oriented professionals.

To insure their own security and welfare, teachers have organized into effective movements via the National Education Association and its many affiliates at the state and local levels or through the labor-affiliated American Federation of Teachers. The NEA, with more than a million members draws more heavily from the rural and suburban schools, whereas the AFT-CIO has attracted the rank and file of the large city school workers. Currently the bargaining agents representing either of these giant organizations—it is hard to distinguish between them today—are negotiating wages and hours, in-service training, curriculum, even discipline with their local school boards. In their headlong pursuit to protect and advance the interests of the teacher, both the NEA and the AFT-CIO have diminished their efforts to promote excellence in their work as educators and have lost public support and respect for the cause of public education.

The story of teachers striking and picketing has become a commonplace news item throughout the country since the record-breaking strike of New York City teachers in 1967. Teachers striking for improvement of their own working conditions have been quick to exploit the stranded students for their own purposes. Signs carried in the picket lines have read: "Teachers Want What Children Need" and "Teachers Want a Chance to Teach." It is true that insecure, unrewarded, and unhappy teachers may be more of a threat than a help to children in the classroom. Unfortunately, the plight of the student does not seem to diminish after the signing of contracts between negotiators. And who is negotiating for the student?

Few school systems take time to inform their young clients of their rights and their guarantee of due process. A bill of rights written by and for students may not solve the crisis in the schools, but it can go a long way to insure for the students a safe, sane, and potentially productive learning environment. The obsequious and passive student of yesteryear, who felt himself at the mercy of the teacher and the school administration, is rapidly becoming aware of his own rights as a human being and as an active, self-directing learner. The lessons learned from the striking teachers, who have taken their case to the streets, have not been lost on the students burdened with mounting grievances.

Reading Silberman, it is not difficult to understand how and why this youthful declaration of independence has been provoked. One can only wonder why the uprising was so long in coming. During recent years the American Civil Liberties Union has constituted the one *friend in court* that has come to the defense of the young students harassed by school administration. For example, the Massachusetts CLU made strong appeals to the school authorities to stop suspending students wearing long hair until the appeals courts have had their final say in the matter. The hair cases were fiercely fought by the Massachusetts Association of School Superintendents and the State Secondary Principals Association. Similar incidents involving dress as well as hair have taken place in all sections of the country. They press home the fact that the school exists for administrators, not for learners, in spite of the lack of any evidence concerning a negative relationship between length of hair and learning.

Earlier, schools were described as *Big Business*. School budgets sustain a wide variety of commercial interests, as even a casual visit to the exhibition halls at the Atlantic City meetings of the American Association of School Administrators will demonstrate. Exactly how much influence and control textbook publishers and manufacturers exercise on what goes on in the classroom to improve and promote better learning is difficult to determine. That the influence is considerable can hardly be denied. Lay and professional workers who have served on school building committees, curriculum and textbook committees, or who are responsible for ordering supplies and equipment are familiar with the sale pitch as to what will work better and insure pupil attention and learning. The purchase of one reading series may center reading instruction around a phonetic system, while another series may set school practice around a more visual approach to reading. The purchase of particular basic texts in science may commit classroom practice to assigning, memorizing, and hearing lessons or to the individual discovery method of instruction. School suppliers are dependent upon school budgets for their existence, but schools often depend upon the manufacturer when it comes to questions concerning how a pupil will sit, what he will learn, and how his achievements will be recorded.

Even local, state, and federal governments have their expectations concerning the aims, methods, and content of instruction. Priorities are indicated in such areas as modern language, science, mathematics, drug education, physical education and other subjects in order to insure an early flight to the moon, the preservation of our form of democracy, and an available labor pool. And at the same time, by extending school requirements, youth can be kept from glutting the labor market.

To hold that school exists for the students and to serve their needs is to establish a high priority for the young learner—a priority that is frequently shunted aside by the needs of teachers, school administrators, professional associations, business interests and local, state and federal governments. Vested interests can and do push student needs to lower priority.

Fantasy:
The School Is Concerned with the Whole Child

It is generally recognized that every youngster brings his early home and family life experiences with him to school. Although the major function of the school is in the area of cognitive development it assumes some responsibility for the youngster's social, emotional, and physical development. The school realizes that cognitive learning does not take place in a vacuum but is a function of the total personality and the social setting. Thus home and community pressures result in school programs for feeding pupils, providing showers and baths, offering drug education, making medical, dental, and nursing services available. In crisis neighborhoods police and firemen guard the staff, the pupils, and the building.

The community school is now running the risk of becoming an omnibus agency serving all the needs of all the pupils and their families. There are obvious limits to what the community school can do within the boundaries of its major function (cognitive development), the qualifications of its trained staff, its physical facilities, and its financial resources. The development of community centers to deliver many services to children, as recommended by the Joint Commission of Mental Health of Children, would alleviate the omnibus role that schools are often forced to play and enable them to return to their more limited and reasonable goals. Perhaps the school has been much too ready to pick up any and all jobs that have been dropped by other agencies such as the family, church, and clinic. The temptation to turn to the school is great, for all the children of all the people are included within this institution. But schools are not hospitals, they are not warehouses in which to store children for a period of time, they are not churches, nor are they merely parks in which to play. If the intellectual elements of school are diminished in any way, then the school becomes less a school.

Fantasy:
The School Provides
for Individual Differences

Enrollment statistics for 1969 indicate that there were 45,618,578 pupils in American classrooms, each with unique backgrounds and unique needs. There were 2,013,836 teachers, with an average salary of $8,840, staffing the classrooms. Like their students, the teachers are also different; they have differing living and teaching styles.

The major preoccupation of school boards and school administrators during the past six decades has not been centered on the educational processes that so preoccupy Silberman. Rather the concern has been for buildings to house the pupils, teachers to staff the classrooms, and money to run the schools. Fulfillment of the American Dream to educate all children in a mass system of free public education, provided little lead time for careful planning of course content and methodology. One result was to standardize the curriculum and to prepare cook books filled with teaching recipes to meet the needs of the invading hordes of children with differing backgrounds and needs. The wonder is that all pupils were accommodated and that enough teachers were trained and recruited.

To house the growing school population, larger and larger edifices were constructed. In the less populated suburban and rural areas schools were regionalized and rationalized in the name of economy and efficiency. The little red school house gave way to the large and impersonal structures housing thousands of pupils. But bigness breeds frustration and aggression.

Most youngsters who enter school today are immediately absorbed into a massive system. Although the school accepts all children, it does so on its own terms. These terms frequently demand some renunciation of differences—personal, social, and cultural—and a constant submission to the processes of conformity and standardization. Most schools achieve their goals at the price of some loss of privacy, personal identity, and individuality. Bigness requires a submission to external rule and regulation and to the pressures of the peer group. Children and youth who are unwilling or unable to submit to the demands of bigness frequently join the ranks of the school failures, the troubled and troublesome, the truants, and the drop-outs. For them the school has served to weaken and destroy the ego. Having gone beyond the critical mass, the American school has shifted from an ego-supporting to an ego-threatening system.

The City of Brockton, Massachusetts, has recently completed the largest and most costly high school on the East Coast. Bringing the 5000 young people to this one learning center skirts the problems of mass control, bureaucracy, impersonality, and anonymity, as is reflected by statements of two troubled seniors. Writing to the editor of the *Brockton Enterprise* in the issue of March 27, 1971, one student complained of the humiliations she suffered in the school, concluding with the suggestion that "members of the school committee and the administration should hold four assembly programs—one for each class—to listen to the students face to face . . . hearing complaints and suggestions for a better atmosphere." Similarly, another student wrote to the same newspaper telling how she and other students felt about being regulated and "hemmed in" by arbitrary rules. "I am a senior and won't be around next year but there will be 5,000 others who will have to put up with the school longer than I have. I pity them. If the students are pressured, restricted, and punished they will rebel and be angry young people. If they have freedom they will learn to accept responsibility and become happy and useful people."(1)

Almost every school provides positive reinforcement for conformity and standardization; schools tend to discourage deviancy as expressed in idiosyncratic personal realization and self development. Deviancy invariably carries a negative connotation. Schools tend to minimize differences by reinforcing conformity and by gearing the curriculum to the modal group and by evaluating performance against median performance at age or grade level.

When individual differences occur in the extreme, as with mentally retarded or emotionally disturbed students, the school tends to recognize and to handle the differences with a vengeance. It tends to magnify and distort the differences by elaborate testing, diagnosing, labeling, and isolating the child for special treatment. In a sense the schools seem to make up for their neglect of individual differences in the normal spread of the school population by overreacting and exaggerating the differences of those youngsters whose extreme exceptionality cannot be denied. Segregating these children for special treatment reinforces a negative self-concept. It also tends to project a self-fulfilling prophecy. Once labeled as *mentally retarded, delinquent* or *disturbed*, the young student knows how he is expected to behave and generally he accommodates.

How to recognize individual differences and assist the young learner to realize himself remains a major problem in mass education. Silberman's complaints concerning the lockstepping of pupils and the disregard of important differences among them are well taken. In the United States we need to face the reality that we may have undertaken an impossible task of meeting individual differences through a system of inadequately financed compulsory mass education.

Fantasy:
Classroom Innovations
Will Result in
Improved Service to Pupils

Gadgets, gimmicks, and special methods follow one another in rapid succession in keeping with the latest educational fad. The long list of new methods and materials which have received attention, enjoyed considerable acceptance, and some of which are now forgotten, raises the question: "How long will the informal and open classroom stay in style?"

We can be sure that the Leicestershire Plan—like the Dalton Plan and the Winnetka Plan—will be replaced. It is only a matter of time. A more basic question is "Will Silberman have any lasting effect on the American classrooms and on teacher training?" Judging from the rise and fall of innovations, the betting odds would indicate, "Very little." Since professional educators are now under pressure to make radical changes to meet current school crises, it is possible that Silberman's proposals will find wide acceptance among the educators and that more permanent changes may result.

Historically, specialized materials and methods have often served as symbols of change and have tended to camouflage the fact that it is business as usual at the same old stand. But gadgetry and new methodologies have tended to pervert pedagogy by promising, for example, to double reading rates with improved comprehension, to make mathematics meaningful and even "easy", and to individualize instantly the learning and teaching processes. One may note, however, that the advertisement of *teacher-proof* courses of study packaged by the Educational Development Corporation of Cambridge, Massachusetts, came to an abortive halt as the need for teacher training emerged with the preliminary classroom tryout.

With the passage of the Elementary and Secondary Education Act schools bought up a lot of electronic equipment, much of which stands idle today. The rapid mushroomlike growth of firms producing auto-instructional devices including *teaching machines* for the push-button or automated classroom was followed by their rapid demise after the first wave of purchase and tryout. As Silberman states, the classroom still looks like the same old shop and the teacher is still standing in front of the class assigning and hearing lessons as the new equipment gathers dust if it has been uncrated. Unfortunately, it appears that making materials and methods available to the classroom teacher does not automatically mean that they will be integrated within the school program.

Fantasy:
Reorganization of the School
Will Improve Teaching and Learning

For a long time schools have been looking for the *right* number combinations for grouping students by age and grade. The current pleasure and promise in school organization involves the concept of *the middle school.* Perhaps this is in anticipation of Silberman's complaint concerning the traditional junior high school as a *cesspool.* The winning number combinations today are 5-3-4 or 4-4-4-. The grade combinations that have proven popular in the past but which are being discarded include: 8-4, 6-2-4, 6-3-3, 6-6, and if you wish to include the junior college, other combinations are possible. Obviously, the formula for permutation and combinations can be used to yield many other organizational sets and, just as obviously, there is no sure route to improved schooling merely by drawing new grade combinations.

Even though the topic of new school organizations will always help attract at least two or three discussion groups at the annual sessions of school administrators, the tendency today is to confuse the issue further with the introduction of the notion of the nongraded classroom as a partial answer to the traditional organization of grades. We can throw in the variable of sex differences, since achievement of girls of a given age is known to vary from the achievement of boys in the same age bracket. Hence, we can introduce more variables and insure more discussion papers at educational conferences. Unfortunately, there is little evidence that would lead us to expect a solution to Silberman's *junior high school cesspool* problem via the number route. Even the extension of the open and informal classroom, so highly touted in Silberman's volume, needs to be carefully checked to make sure that the open classroom in any combination of grades does not remain an *empty* classroom. How to maintain and fill the open classroom as a continuous, rich, and varied learning experience within any organizational structure is the pay-off question.

There is a danger that the open and informal classroom will be foisted on all teachers and pupils regardless of their learning or teaching styles. Teachers should be free to select their own methodology as long as they can show increments of learning. There is evidence in studies of nursery school children indicating that some structure is needed until the child learns to adapt to changes without undue anxiety and confusion which can arise when pressures of self-determination and self-direction push the child beyond his competencies. Many older children, and some of my own graduate students, who have always been told what to do, when to do it, how to do it, and whether it has been done "right" resist and resent the lack of structure.

Fantasy:
The P.T.A. Is a Helpful
Organization to Have around a School

Surprisingly, Silberman pays little attention to parents. I could find only minor emphasis on parent-involvement and only the most fleeting reference (page 289) to the time-worn if not time-honored P.T.A. How can one ignore the twelve million members of the National Congress of Parents and Teachers? I must confess that Silberman's omission fits my prejudice toward the P.T.A. as a waste of time as currently organized and directed.

Nevertheless, Silberman's recommendations for improving classroom practices and teacher training might stand a better chance of implementation if the local, regional, state, and national P.T.A. units could be enlisted in his crusade. I have come to view the National Congress of Parents and Teachers as the most unused and misused human resource in the country and have at times attempted to point to ways to harness the potential of this giant organization.

Some Pedagogic
Echoes from the Past

After indulging in these popular fantasies, let me return to my own personal realities. Turning the pages of *Crisis in the Classroom* dredged up some of my own past writings and left me with an empty feeling that I have long been whistling in the dark. A few selected examples which anticipated Silberman will explain my reaction.

In 1945 I described a large sample of delinquents in New Jersey who had found their own kind of Hell in school and who lived in constant frustration.(2) The evidence indicated that schools can cause overaggressive behavior aimed at people and property as well as self. A significant drop-off in the summer rates of delinquency was noted annually when school was not in session.

In 1958 attention was directed to the cover or *hidden* curriculum which has more to do with success and failure than the formal and overt curriculum of the classroom.(3)

In the 30th Yearbook of the National Council for the Social Studies concern was voiced for the passive dependency in which American youth were kept in the schools and classrooms. Youth did not have a function and schools were not providing the maturing experiences that would insure the emergence of self-directing adults.(4)

In 1965 I pointed out the dilemma in role conflict that teachers must face in maintaining standards and in helping the young student, particularly when working with those youngsters whose value systems differed markedly from that of the school and of the dominant society.(5)

After working on the UNESCO youth desk and reviewing youth programs in school and out-of-school in twelve countries, I was forced to conclude that the relationships between adults and youth would result in serious confrontations and end in revolt and rebellion. I was not aware of how soon this would happen in the United States.(6)

There have been many voices in the past crying out in the wilderness of the Black Board Jungles and in the Suburban Sanctuaries. But, lacking both patron and press agent, these voices were unheard and the educational prophets died like muted, inglorious Miltons.

Accepting Dewey as a *given,* the following individuals from an early generation are mostly disregarded by Silberman although they were among the first to break ground: Charles H. Judd, Boyd H. Bode, William H. Kilpatrick, William C. Bagley, Harold Rugg, William H. Burton, Hollis L. Caswell, W. W. Charters, Edward L. Thorndike, William S. Gray, I. L. Kandel, Paul R. Mort, George D. Strayer, George D. Stoddard, Carleton Washburne, Lewis M. Terman, Gardner Murphy, and Caroline Zachry—to name but a few. The tap roots of Silberman's major thesis can be traced back to this earlier generation of educational thought and reformation rather than to the contemporary generation to which Silberman is more heavily footnoted. I could locate only a fleeting nod to five of these primary sources. The serious student of the educational crisis who reviews the contributions made by these authorities will be rewarded by discovering how much had been anticipated of the present problems, needs, and solutions.

In these critical times it is refreshing to hear the trumpet sound resurrecting the forgotten and the dead in the call to insure the salvation of the American public schools. Perhaps the crisis is over and the schools are beyond salvation.

Notes

1. Quoted with permission of the students, Donna Wolfe and Roberta Lane, and the publishers of *The Brockton Enterprise.*
2. W. C. Kvaraceus, *Juvenile Delinquency and the School* (Yonkers, N.Y.: World Book Co., 1945), p. 135.
3. W. C. Kvaraceus, "The Behavioral Deviate in the Culture of the Secondary School," in *Frontiers of Secondary Education, III,* ed. Paul M. Halverson (Syracuse, N.Y.: Syracuse University Press, 1958), pp. 18-27.
4. W. C. Kvaraceus, "Tomorrow's Youth and Tomorrow's Citizens," in *Citizenship and a Free Society: Education for the Future,* 30th Yearbook of the National Council for the Social Studies, ed. Franklin Patterson (Washington, D. C.: National Council for the Social Studies, 1960), p. 20.
5. W. C. Kvaraceus, "Negro Youth and Social Adaptation: the Role of the School as an Agent of Change," *Negro Self Concept* (New York: McGraw Hill Book Co., 1965), p. 111.
6. W. C. Kvaraceus, *Dynamics of Delinquency* (Columbus, Ohio: Charles E. Merrill, Inc., 1966), p. 250.

VIII

Response

Charles E. Silberman

Since both space and time are short, let me dispense with unnecessary rhetoric by way of introduction, and simply say that I am deeply honored and flattered that the National Society for the Study of Education has commissioned this volume, and that eight men of such distinction have taken the time and trouble to write the critical essays contained here.

It seems to me that the various criticisms my eight critics make can be usefully grouped in two broad categories. The first involves sins of commission: a number of the critics argue that I am wrong in what I say—wrong in my diagnosis of the nature of the crisis, or in the solutions I propose. The second category involves sins of omission: according to these criticisms, the book is marred by my failure to raise, or to adequately come to grips with, certain kinds of questions.

Sins of Commission

Let me deal first with the sins of commission.

1. The most sweeping criticism is the one which James Koerner makes:—that my picture of the American public schools is so badly exaggerated and overdrawn as to be essentially false and misleading.

Although this hardly constitutes an adequate response to Koerner's charge, I find it interesting and significant that he is the only one to make this charge. The other seven critics, as well as the authors of the previously published book reviews reprinted here, all accept my basic picture of what the schools are like. And while the grounds for Koerner's disagreement certainly are consistent with the positions he has taken in the past, I confess some wry amusement in the fact that Jim Koerner is berating Charles Silberman for being too unkind to, and insufficiently appreciative of, the American public schools and American public school teachers and administrators. I had not previously classified him as one of the defenders of the status quo! Nor do his published criticisms of the schools and of the schools of education leave the impression that he sees the glass half full rather than half empty.

But how could I persuade Koerner that I am correct, that American schools really *are* "grim, repressive, joyless places"? He regards that judgment as an "unqualified assertion" from which the rest of the book flows. And he rejects my "evidence"—the quotation marks are his—as "flamboyant 'items' listed in a supposedly objective fashion, the suggestion being that they are representative samples, when they might be quite extraordinary samples, if not caricatures. . ." He continues: "The trouble with such evidence . . . is that the reader would be helpless to evaluate it, and of necessity would be thrown back on his personal experience. So it is with Silberman's book. What else can one do but accept it on faith or reject it on the basis of what one considers common sense? No firm evidence (this time the word appears without quotes) appears in the book for or against Silberman's principal claims and theories. What appears are anecdotes, impressions, beliefs, assertions, and points of view."

It is not clear to me what kind of evidence (or "evidence") Koerner would accept. The critical question involves the nature of evidence: if personal experience is to be ruled out, along with anecdotes reflecting that experience, how *does* one make a judgment about the schools?

I stand on my judgments. As indicated in the book, they grow out of my own observations, together with the observations of three research associates, in public schools in every part of the country and serving every socio-economic, racial, and ethnic group. And our judgments are supplemented by the judgments which a great many other scholarly and journalistic observers have made—most particularly, Philip Jackson and John Goodlad. These judgments are supported in this volume in William Kvaraceus' paper, among others.

If I had had any doubts about the validity of my judgments, however, they would have been relieved by the response to my book. I have had the experience in almost every part of the country of having parents, students, teachers, and administrators refer to specific "items" and insist that they *know* that the item in question occurred in their school. In no case in which this has happened, have the people been correct. My items and other descriptions would seem to have an even greater universality than I had realized.

2. A second error, according to Mark Shedd and Terry Borton, is that I describe the wrong crisis. Thus, they write that *"Crisis In The Classroom* hardly mentions the immediate crises that we and many other educators face daily: a yearly battle for funds to keep from closing the schools; a bloody clash between four thousand black students and the city police; sixteen simultaneous racial attacks at one high school; a teachers' strike so bitter that striking teachers would no longer talk to those who came in to teach the kids; forty-seven boys killed in gang warfare in our city last year; thirteen-year-old kids dying of drugs. These crises, which are front-page news, are as disturbing as they are visible—at least as disturbing as the evidence that Silberman amasses to support his charge that 'schools are the kind of institution one cannot really dislike until one gets to know them well.' "

I would have to argue that most of the immediate crises that Shedd and Borton and most other public school administrators face grow out of the crisis on which I concentrated, the grimness, joylessness, and sheer destructiveness of most schools. The bitterness of teacher strikes has much to do with the fact that schools are destructive of teachers as well as of students; and while racial conflict in the schools obviously reflects the racial tensions of the larger society, such conflict is exacerbated by the destructive ways in which schools traditionally and typically deal with black or other minority group or lower class students (see Chapter three of *Crisis In The Classroom*).

I plead guilty, however, to the charge of not having tried to describe all of the crises of American society. I attempted in my foreward and in Chapter Two to indicate how the educational crisis I was dealing with related to the other and larger crises of American society as a whole; to have tried to deal with every problem of the schools, let alone of American society, would have made it impossible for me to deal adequately with any of them. And I have dealt with other crises in my other writings.

3. The real point of this criticism of Shedd and Borton is to build up to a third criticism, which they and John Mann make: that my explanation of the crisis is inadequate or incorrect, that mindlessness is *not* the central problem.

This is the most important, and as Professor Mann states it, the most telling criticism to emerge from the various essays. I confess that Mann draws blood when he charges me with having "the liberal's humanistic faith that if people would only think seriously they would all turn out to want the same thing, or at least to have compatible purposes." I plead guilty; I am afraid that I did assume, somewhat mindlessly, that serious thought about purpose *would* tend to produce some reasonable consensus in favor of a more humane approach to education and schooling.

But not entirely so! There are passages in the foreward and afterword which imply that thought about purpose may not automatically lead to people wanting the same thing. Thus, I wrote that:

My motive is political, in the broadest sense of the term—as George Orwell defined it, "to push the world in a certain direction, to alter other people's ideas of the kind of society that they should strive after." I do not expect that all will agree with me; I hope that all will find my meaning clear, and thereby be moved to clarify their own thinking.(p. vii)

But Mann is essentially correct in his criticism; most of the book does assume implicitly that if people will only think about educational purpose, they will all want the same thing.

My error may lie more in letting this assumption be implicit, however, than in the assumption itself. My experience since the book was published suggests that conflict over goals may be less than Mann, or Shedd and Borton, think—that more people may be amenable to persuasion than they assume. Certainly my criticisms of the schools and my proposals for reform have received far more acceptance than I had expected or even had dared hope for, among teachers, administrators, teacher organizations, parents, and the general public.

My experience also suggests that much more of the strife that we are experiencing—strife that appears to be derived from fundamentally conflicting purposes—can be reduced by serious thought and discussion than I might have expected. In public lectures and in radio and television appearances, for example, I have found that surprising numbers of people whom we classify, for want of a better term, as *middle America,* can be persuaded to support a freer, more open, and more humane approach to education. Not all, certainly, for there *are* conflicts of values that are not likely to be resolved by discussion; I doubt that I can persuade Jim Koerner that informal education is to be preferred to formal instruction, and I am *certain* that I cannot persuade Mortimer Smith. And it would be fruitless to try to persuade William Shockley or George Wallace that black students' low scores on standardized tests are the result of the kinds of schooling they receive rather than their genetic inferiority. And, of course, there are conflicts of interest in a political as well as a value sense.

This bears on the other part of Mann's, and Shedd and Borton's, criticism: that the problem is not mindlessness, but rather mindfulness. As Shedd and Borton write, "No one who faces crises daily can believe, as Silberman does, that 'mindlessness is the central problem.' For situations do not reach the crisis stage unless someone 'minds' what is happening, unless systems of meaning are threatened, unless purposes are in conflict." Or as Mann writes:

What goes on in our schools is as much the result of shrewd intent as it is the result of mindlessness. . . . The mindlessness is not all that mindless, the evil not all that benign, and the oppressiveness that characterizes our schools not all that accidental. Holt is glib, no doubt, in his vision of teachers as conspirators against children. But Silberman is equally glib, I think, in his denial that the badness of schooling has any systemic or intentional dimensions at all.

Perhaps. Yet Mann concedes that "the intent, of course, is rarely the overt intent to treat children destructively." This concession is crucial, or so it seems to me: to define the problem as mindlessness is to argue that there is no *they* who want children destroyed. Of course there are individual teachers and administrators who are harsh, mean, vindictive, racist, and so on; there is no reason to assume that education will have a substantially smaller proportion of such people than medicine or the law or social work or any other profession. The point is that the deliberately cruel or destructive people are in the minority. The critical word is *deliberately,* or as Mann puts it, with "overt intent." To repeat Mann's qualification, "the intent is rarely the overt intent to treat children destructively." When teachers do treat children destructively, it is because they have been caught up in a system that is destructive of them as well as of the students. The great majority of teachers would rather be kind than cruel, would rather succeed than fail.

In fairness to Mann, he qualifies his qualification. After denying that the overt intent is to treat children destructively, he adds, "But the system required to serve certain interests *is* in fact destructive of children, and the fact that we have such a system at the very best reflects a perverse sense of priorities."

I agree that we have a perverse sense of priorities; again, the question is one of intent. We agree that there is no collective *they;* but Mann goes on to speak of *the system* which requires the destruction of children—a system which itself is "required to serve certain interests."

I have trouble identifying the interests that require the destruction of children. Nor do I think that *the system,* in the sense of American society as a whole, requires the destruction of children, or any other aspects of the way schools are now organized. On the contrary, American society is far more open and far less authoritarian than the schools themselves. Even on an automobile assembly line, there are coffee breaks; more important, the workers are organized. To the extent to which the system of the schools requires that they be as they now are, it is the mindlessness that is characteristic of most or all bureaucratic institutions; that is, the fact that the perpetuation of the system takes precedence over the fulfillment of the goals for which the system was initially established. Bureaucratic institutions, in Peter F. Drucker's phrase, prefer to do things the right way than to do the right things.

My conviction that the problem is mindlessness also grows out of the logic of the argument as a whole. In an earlier draft, the tone of the book was closer to that of my fellow critics of the schools. At a meeting of the members of my Advisory Commission, Robert Merton suggested that the draft contained a basic contradiction. As he put it, I was taking a Rousseauian view of children but a Hobbesian view of teachers; he suggested that I could not have it both ways—that I would have to decide which view of human nature and its potential I accepted. If I believed that children were innately good and tended to fulfill the expectations held out for them, it was illogical to argue or imply that teachers were innately bad. Informal education implicitly if not explicitly contains a Rousseauian view of children; it is illogical, to say the least, to argue that case and then hold to a Hobbesian or conspiratorial view of teachers as the villains. And if I seem to argue the Rousseauian view too strongly, I would also plead artistic license. After all the conspiratorial theories of recent years, it seemed important to argue (and hopefully establish the fact) that teachers are *not* the villains, that on the contrary they are as much sinned against as sinning. The affirmative response to my book from most teacher organizations, as well as from individual teachers, would seem to justify this view.

4. Lastly, several of the writers point to what they view as mistakes or inadequacies in the solutions I propose.

(a) Here, again, Professor Mann draws blood in suggesting that I have not given adequate attention to what he calls the "developmental dimension" of purposefulness in the lives of students, and the complex relation between the acceptance of purpose from the teacher and the emergence of the student's own purpose. I suspect that he is correct, therefore, in suggesting that I have slighted the importance of the *bull session* as "a critical transitional stage in the process from mindlessly accepting the mindlessness of a school system to discovering and acting upon one's own sense of purpose." At the same time, however, I think that Mann underestimates the dangers of the bull session becoming entrenched—of students and teachers becoming so enamoured with their new freedom to talk about what interests and concerns *them* that they never get past this essentially narcissistic stage, and so never get to see that intellectual discipline can be useful in solving or illuminating problems of personal interest.

But this last view is what Mann cannot accept; ultimately we disagree over the relation between freedom, discipline, and structure because I do operate out of what Mann calls "a fundamentally conservative view of epistemology and of schooling." I *do* believe that one piece of learning is not as good as any other, that some things are more worth knowing than others, that knowing one thing is not the same as knowing another; that is why schools exist. If it did not matter what students learn, if there were no importance attached to bringing students into contact with the culture, there would be no need for them to go to school—certainly no need great enough to offset the disadvantages of schooling. As Harris Wofford has written about his unhappy experiences as President of the State University of New York College at Old Westbury, "If everyone is free to do his own thing, the college (or school) cannot be free to do *its* thing."(1)

I find it useful in this context to follow David Hawkins' distinction between the *curriculum* and the *syllabus*. As Hawkins defines it, the curriculum is socially determined: in every culture, there are certain things which every person must know, at a minimum, in order to function. In American culture, that means mastery of the skills of literacy and mathematics, some understanding of science, some understanding of the history of the United States and of Western and non-Western cultures. While the curriculum is socially determined, the syllabus, as Hawkins defines it, should—must—be left to the individual teacher and his or her students, for the syllabus concerns the ways in which the specific students in a specific class will learn the broad subject matter of the curriculum. There is no one way, no best way, to learn history or physics or mathematics or, for that matter, how to read and write. In determining the syllabus, the teacher should—must—take individual students' individual purposes into account. The point is that it *is* possible to give considerable rein to individual students' individual purposes without sacrificing or unduly subordinating the teachers' or the schools' purposes.

(b) Mann also raises an important question about my conviction that "it can happen here": as he points out, the American reforms to which I point have been instituted by educators who possess extraordinary energy and talent. It is quite reasonable, therefore, to question whether their results *depend* upon their extraordinary talents. As Mann writes, "The question is not how many more programs can Lillian Weber run, but rather how far the quality will spread beyond the reach of her direct energies, and how much will the quality deteriorate with increased distance and time. For surely it is an idle hope to think we are likely soon to have enough Lillian Webers to go around."

I think an honest answer must be that the beginnings of the new reform movement have depended on the genius of the Lillian Webers, Vito Perrones, et al. This much conceded, however, it should be pointed out that genius has turned out to be a good deal more widespread than any of us might have expected. The extraordinary people who are responsible for the introduction of informal education have, so to speak, come out of the educational woodwork. Vito Perrone, after all, is at the University of North Dakota, not Harvard, or Teachers College, or Stanford (and he came to North Dakota from Northern Michigan State University); Lillian Weber was an obscure, untenured assistant professor of Early Childhood Education at City College when she began her program; Marie Hughes was teaching at the University of Arizona and is now at the University of New Mexico; except for her reputation among some mathematics curriculum reformers, Lore Rasmussen was not well known before she began working in the Philadelphia schools; and although her reputation was beginning to spread among New York City teachers, Martha Froelich's achievements had not been publicized. It is surely significant that genius has been discovered in what an Ivy Leaguer would call the boondocks rather than in the centers of so-called academic excellence; if this much talent has emerged so rapidly, I think it is reasonable to assume that there is a great deal more still waiting to be discovered.

A good deal of it has already surfaced; if I were drawing up a list of unusually talented informal educators today, I would add, among others, such people as Herb Mack and Ann Cook in New York, Marian Taylor and Pat Carini in North Bennington, Vermont, Virgil M. Howes of the International Center for Educational Development in Encino, California, Henry Gallina in Lompoc, California, Celia Haughton at the Convent of the Sacred Heart Junior School in Greenwich, Connecticut, Elwyn Richardson, now at the Mountain View Center for Environmental Education at the University of Colorado, Ernestine Rouse in Philadelphia, to name just a few. And I have met or have had correspondence with individual teachers and principals in every part of the country who are moving toward informal education with what appears to be intelligence and serious thought.

None of this, of course, directly answers Mann's question of whether a movement initiated by extraordinary talent will take root where the talents are more ordinary; the answer lies in the future. For the moment, one can say that there is no reason to believe that quality must deteriorate with increased distance and time, and there is considerable reason to believe that such deterioration can be avoided.

Sins of Omission

Let me turn now to the sins of omission with which I am charged. David Goslin has provided a generous context within which to consider this group of errors. On the one hand, he writes, "It is always unfair to attack an author for not writing the book you hoped he would write," but "on the other hand, the potential effectiveness of the book Mr. Silberman *did* write is . . . reduced as a consequence of the things it fails to take into account." Fair enough.

1. Goslin argues that I give too little weight to the social and cultural environment in which the school is situated.

Although Mr. Silberman acknowledges the importance of such influences at various points throughout his book, his primary focus on the classroom leads him away from a thorough analysis of their impact on the learning process itself and on the problems of achieving educational reform in very different social settings. By drawing upon examples of informal education in a variety of English schools as well as a few in this country ("item: a classroom in a school in a coal mining town in Yorkshire . . ."), he gives us the impression that the necessary techniques are similar from one school to the next and, more important, require only a willingness to try on the part of teachers and administrators . . .

Goslin goes on to argue that family characteristics, peer group norms, communities, etc. cannot be ignored. "To take a trivial example, enriching the learning environment is almost certain to require different kinds of materials in rural schools as opposed to urban ghetto schools if the interest of children is to be aroused initially and maintained over time."

Amitai Etzioni makes much the same criticism in his essay review in the *Harvard Educational Review*. He writes;

The concept of the same school structure for all never had any broad reality in a society where children come from such divergent starting points. . . . Nor has the notion of one school for all, on the face of it a greater equality, any normative validity. "Informality for all" is no more realistic than assuming you can teach all fifth graders the same math just because the Piaget scheme suggests that they all ought to be "ready" for it.

I am frankly puzzled: Goslin and Etzioni are criticizing me for saying something I do not think I said, or even implied. On the contrary, it seems to me that the substance of my argument runs the other way.

Let me deal with the substantive issue, however, rather than with the question of what I wrote or did not write. Nothing in informal education as I understand it can be interpreted as calling for "the same school structure for all." The reverse is the case: in an informal school, the teacher *must* take account of the realities of family background, ethnicity, race, and socio-economic background, because the teacher's starting point is the individual child—what he is, what he knows, what he likes and what he dislikes, what interests him and what does not interest him, and so on. As Anne M. Bussis and Edward A. Chittenden of Educational Testing Service have written, one of the critical assumptions of informal education is that;

the children constitute the basic resources of the educational process. In contrast to those educational theories which *assume* the presence of a child during instruction, the informal approach *requires* the presence of the child to define instruction. Teaching begins with the assumption that the children coming into the classroom come with capabilities and experiences—shared and unique—and it is the teacher's job to see that those resources give a direction and meaning to learning.(2)

If teachers are to deal with students as individuals—with their uniqueness as well as what they have in common—if students constitute the most basic resource of the educational process, then teachers must take social and cultural factors into account insofar as they affect the educational process. But *only* insofar as they affect the educational process! Perhaps this is the critical point of difference between me and Professor Etzioni in particular; if I read him correctly, he *knows* that students from lower class homes need a very different kind of education than middle class students; I am not so sure. Etzioni sees individual or group differences as a problem; the informal educators whose work I describe see individual and group differences as an opportunity—as the very stuff of learning. Far from denying differences, they prize them.

The point is that the teacher in an informal classroom has the entire range of classroom practices at his or her disposal. If a student needs a great deal of formal, even rigid, structure, the teacher is free to provide as much structure (or as much rigidity) as the child needs. If a child needs direct instruction, the teacher is free to provide it. And so it goes. The teacher can and indeed is expected to respond to each student's individual needs, whether those needs grow out of too much poverty or too much affluence. But the teacher is dealing with live children, not with stereotyped culturally deprived or culturally disadvantaged children. To repeat, teachers take account of social and cultural phenomena to the extent—but *only* to the extent—to which these factors are relevant in the classroom, that is, to the extent to which they affect the kinds of children who are in *this* particular classroom at *this* particular time. To take account of social and cultural factors in any other way may be to distort the educational process. I agree with the view of a principal whom Robert Coles quotes in *Teachers and the Children of Poverty:*

In a way, a lot of our teachers, in a progressive school system like this, have learned too much sociology and psychology—or maybe learned to use what they've learned in a very self-defeating way. They read and read and take extra courses on Negro history or whatever, and then they take all the phrases they've picked up and do all the same things with them that supposedly ignorant people do with blunter words—discount and discredit and even slightly insult black people. It's not easy to say something like that, but I see it happening, *hear* it happening all the time.

2. A number of writers, particularly David Goslin and John Mann criticize my failure to analyze in any detail the social and political processes through which the kinds of reform I advocate can be achieved. As Goslin puts it,

Mr. Silberman clings to the optimistic view that demonstrating to a person the error of his ways and giving him a vision of something better will produce a change in his behavior. It is well known, however, that change, especially at the institutional level, requires a great deal more than desire and good will on the part of isolated individuals. By neglecting political and organizational features of our schools and school systems, along with the larger social context in which they are embedded, Mr. Silberman fails in his ultimate task: to provide clear-cut means by which social theory can be translated into public policy.

I plead Guilty With An Explanation. It is true that I did not indicate in any detail how the reforms I propose can be implemented. But to the extent to which this omission constitutes a defect, it is an indication how much has changed—how far we have come—in the past year or two. When I began writing, the problem was not *how* but *what* —not how to achieve reform, but what reforms ought to be achieved. To the extent to which discussion of tactics was relevant, it was mainly in terms of how to prevent the wrong reforms from being realized.

The task I set myself—correctly, I still think, in the context in which I was writing—was to define and describe what is wrong with the schools and with teacher education; to say what needs to be done; to demonstrate that what needs to be done *can* be done, that my proposed reforms are practical; and to persuade teachers, administrators, educationists, government officials, philathropoids, and the general public to support these reforms. How these reforms could be achieved appeared to me to be a question that could be dealt with only *after* these prior questions had been answered; given limitations of time and space, I concentrated on the prior questions.

In any case, I did not anticipate the favorable response the book has received—more importantly, the favorable response that the idea of humanizing the educational system has received. It simply did not occur to me (or anyone else) in June of 1970, when I made the final revisions, that less than a year later some advocates of informal education would be worrying about too rapid acceptance of the idea, with the attendant dangers of faddism! This wide acceptance says a lot about the nation's mood and temper, and indirectly, therefore, about the prospects for substantive institutional change.

Notes

1. Harris Wofford, Jr., "Case Study of an Experiment: The New College at Old Westbury," paper given to the Danforth Foundation Workshop on Liberal Arts Education, July 7, 1969 (mimeographed); republished in the *Educational Record,* Winter Issue, 1970.
2. Anne M. Bussis and Edward A. Chittenden, *Analysis of an Approach to Open Education* (Princeton, N. J.: Educational Testing Service, 1970). This brief monograph constitutes the most thoughtful, sensitive, and insightful analysis of what is involved in informal education that I have seen.

Reviews

Review of *Crisis in the Classroom*

Amitai Etzioni

Over the recent decades our ambition to fashion society in the shape of our values has swollen. We no longer accept society as a given, as a pre-existing state of nature. We view it as an arrangement, one which *we* can disassemble and then rearrange. We seek not merely to reform but to transform the relations among the races, the classes, the nations; we seek to deeply affect people's smoking, drug use, drinking, and eating habits, as well as to fundamentally change their education. Our economic, political, and intellectual capacity to affect these changes has increased, but much more slowly than our ambitions. We are now learning, as recent discussions of the "peace dividend" indicated, the full measure of this disparity between ambition and resources. Even if the war is finally terminated and the SALT talks do succeed, there apparently will be available only $15 to $20 new billions per annum for domestic reforms, which require at least $60 to $100 billions. As a nation, it seems, we are much more inclined to talk reform than to display the political will required to bring it about. In those domestic sectors where the nation does find the will and the resources, it frequently lacks the necessary know-how. The knowledge and skills needed to provide a *viable* plan for social engineering are still rudimentary. Frequently we are still guided by well meaning but inadequately conceptualized and poorly worked out blueprints, by semi-utopian programs of which Silberman's book is a recent example.

The problem is not Silberman's, but is a common one shared by most of our efforts at guided societal(1) change. Like several other such books, it is the result of a commission's study, involved extensive interviews, travel, and considerable staff work, and a

Reprinted by permission from *Harvard Educational Review*, 41, Feb. 1971, 87-98. Copyright © 1971 by President and Fellows of Harvard College. Mr. Etzioni is professor of sociology at Columbia University.

$300,000 investment by the Carnegie Corporation. The study provides an opportunity to examine the problems encountered by those who seek to provide an intelligent input into the decisions of policy makers and into public debates as to what is to be done. Similar questions raised by this book can be asked about the designs of the war against poverty, Title I, compensatory education, the Kerner Commission's report, and—more generally—the thinking which preceded and accompanied most of the four hundred odd domestic reform programs initiated in the U.S.A. since the early Sixties. (The limitations encountered by social thinkers of other societies, which include some of ours and some of their own, do not concern us here.)

Blueprints for a societal change may be usefully assessed in terms of: the definition of the problem (why is change needed); the goals subscribed to (where we ought to be); the specificity of the recommendations; the extent to which those are based on empirical evidence and on sound theory; the degree to which the recommendations take into account the linkages between the problem studied and others which inflict the same society, as well as the relationship between the policies recommended for the problem under study and those sought for other sectors of the same society; and the extent to which the analysis is anchored in an encompassing concept of the society and its dynamics.

<u>Definition of the Problem</u> I cannot summarize Silberman's definition of the problem more effectively than Christopher Lehmann-Haupt who wrote:

Mr. Silberman has sailed up the shallow creek of American education, surveyed the landscape and pronounced it joyless, mindless, barren. The natives, he says, are pinched and crabbed, and stand before their children mumbling empty incantations; the children stare back silently, hollow-eyed, and pick their scabs. (*New York Times*, October 8, 1970).

Stylistically, Silberman, like most reform writers, utilizes straight English prose rather than sociologese. He is not reluctant to use terms which have normative and emotive connotations or to cue the reader to his general ideological posture which—unlike that of former Senators Tydings and Goodell—*is* radical-liberal. Typically, Silberman does not seek a revolution and is careful to disassociate himself from the more radical writers such as John Holt, Paul Goodman, and Edgar Z. Friedenberg. At the same time, he asks for *more* than piecemeal, limited reform. He believes that the total educational system of America must be transformed through the accumulation of sweeping, peaceful, and encompassing changes. In the course of these, the nation will be redone, since the ills of education are diagnosed as reflecting and reinforcing those of a society in deep crisis.

As in other such documents, for instance the Report of the Kerner Commission, the definition of the problem is by far the best part of the work. We recognize the symptoms pointed out; the challenge reads well; it arouses the desire to get out there and do something about all these horrors. They all deserve "A" for exhortation.

But these documents do not limit themselves to preaching or to outlining societal symptomatology; they do seek root-causes and they make what look like specific recommendations. Hence, they open themselves to the critique of their value as a guide to deliberate societal change. Silberman suggests that the crisis—education's loss of meaning and authority, and hence its reliance on discipline which *causes* disciplinary problems—results from the *rapid* changing of our world. As a consequence, the nation can no longer draw on an educational system, whose purpose is to transfer the accumulated wisdom of earlier generations. A new system is needed which is highly "horizontal," participatory, and which stresses helping the pupil to evolve procedures for knowing rather than transmitting details. This new system should also focus on the evolution of the whole man rather than preparing manpower for a fragmented life in the obsolescent industrial-bureaucratic society. As I said, the definition of the problem is quite convincing. But what about the plan?

The Purposes of the New Education   Once the ills of the present are recited, setting the goals for the future becomes almost an inevitable step for the radical-liberal writer. But, as several commissions have discovered, setting goals is a very unrewarding enterprise.(2)

The twin traps which await the goal-setters are vagueness and dissensus. To say, as Silberman does repeatedly, that the purpose of education should be to render our society "humane and just" is no more of a guidepost for school boards or community groups than the seven virtues and less so than the ten commandments. On the other hand, to specify what a just or a humane society entails is an inordinately difficult task, and one which would quickly elicit very considerable disagreements among those who are to accept the policy writer's advice.

Once it is recognized that consensus cannot be assumed, the policy writer must ask to what historical, societal, or political force or forces he addresses himself. Silberman and others write as if as long as their counsel is wise and worthy, it will be heeded. Actually, at the moment, there is very little reason to believe that America is headed toward either a humane or a just society or could be so transformed by any educational reforms the present system would tolerate. Why then design an educational system to serve such a transformed society?

While the answer is not to bless wherever the society is going anyhow, the writer whose interests go beyond preaching or fiction must constrain his prescriptions to the confines of where the society might be made to go. He must couple his work to goal-setting processes which grow out of the tensions and dynamics of the society he is addressing. The moralist can advocate anything *he* believes in. However, for societal designers to write policy to their own goals (or to leave undocumented the assumption that their design is relevant to a viable societal, historical force) is to place themselves where God, history, the polity, or "the movement" belong, and to truncate analytic responsibilities.

From the Crisis to Silberman's Future: How to Get There? The test for blueprints of reforms or societal transformations is not the acidity of their critical prolegomena or the placidity of their futuristic poetry but the sharpness of the cutting edge of their recommendations. Sharpness is to be found in making recommendations specific, spelling out the reasons one expects the proposed changes to have the projected impact, and in marshalling the necessary evidence to support such claims. Most blueprint makers escape such detailed specifications for any one of their recommendations, by briefly listing many recommendations. A typical example of this fallacy is the Kerner Commission Report which lists more than a hundred suggestions, none of which are spelled out. Silberman achieves a better balance. His core idea, the informalization of American schools, receives considerable treatment in his book. Many of the numerous recommendations he makes, concerning, for instance, changes in teacher education, follow from or supplement his core idea. How valid is the core conception?

The main features of informal schools, a subject to which we cannot do justice here, are the replacement of the teacher as directing a passively seated class of children, by several "interest areas" in which children *do*, at their own pace, a variety of things *they* are interested in, for varying time intervals, with the help of teachers and teacher-aides. Self-directed, self-disciplined, the children enjoy rather than work at their tasks. The teachers' main duty is to provide a stimulating, encouraging environment. This informalization of the schools entails more than reorganization. Teachers must be re-educated to be able to fulfill their roles in the new classroom. The substance of the curriculum must be adapted to be more meaningful, open to the child's interests, and "balanced" to include the affective next to the cognitive, and esthetics and ethics next to acquiring information and skills.

Informal schools were recommended by the Plowden Report of

Great Britain and are being introduced there. "Open classroom" is a similar, albeit more radical, concept endorsed by a variety of American writers on education and practiced in a few places in this country. The progressive movement harbored a similar idea. Silberman stresses the differences between the idea he endorses, the informalizing schools, and the open or progressive mode of education. In the informal school, he says, the teacher does have a guiding role. Spontaneity, it is recognized, is not all that is needed; encouragement to growth is also to be provided.

Now we turn to the tough test: how valid are the prescriptions? If you come to a society and recommend that its schools (or welfare system, or prisons, or some other major institution) be remade, and your advice is faulty, energies and resources made available to reform will be wasted; frustrations will multiply; and the end result may be as bad or worse than where you started. (Silberman's report on the fate of all pre-Silberman educational reform movements in the U.S.A. provides convincing reading on this subject.) Hence, the responsible designer must be precise enough in his recommendations, so that his ideas can be critically examined and tested. After all, a mere change in the direction of the traffic, as Sweden found out recently, costs millions of dollars and requires considerable other adaptations. Informalizing the American schools, if it can be done, is not much less of an undertaking than the war on poverty and may be an even match to desegregation.

The demand to provide an idea which would make a viable program, let me be the first to admit, is a harsh one. In each area of social endeavor, there are thousands of ideas, hundreds of programs, and, at best, a handful of effective reforms. That is, most ideas do not survive the trip from concept to reality and all are significantly modified on the way. The steps needed to select those ideas which could make viable programs of reconstruction are best depicted in terms of the "R and D" (for "research and development") sequence followed in engineering. In this field, a concept is first concretized into a rough sketch, which is followed by the production of detailed blueprints. These, in turn, are converted into small scale models, which are tested in laboratories. Models which survive these tests provide the basis for one or more full-scale prototypes which are built and tried. In social "engineering," the tendency is still to omit most or all of these stages and to jump from an idea to its implementation in a mass system. In this way, a theoretical postulate was written into the law, which required "maximum feasible participation of the poor," which view turned out to be quite unfeasible. A form of compensatory education for the disadvantaged was awarded $1.2 billion a year over four years under Title I before the Coleman Report, the key relevant research on the possible effects of such a drive, was available.

Silberman's informalize-the-schools offers an idea in the rough-sketch stage. He does point to live systems (in United Kingdom and United States) to support the viability of his plan. However, for reasons which will become evident below, these do *not* provide the test or specificity needed to evaluate the idea of informal schooling. Let me digress long enough to say that there is only so much one man can do, even with $300,000 and a team. Nor am I sorry to see an idea written up. Silberman's book does, though, serve well to illustrate what is needed to advance a process he and many others start, but few care to advance, let alone to complete. How far does Silberman carry the scheme he favors? How specified and documented is his advice?

Specificity   Critical to the whole idea of the informal classroom is the role of the teacher. If he overly exerts his influence by making children learn his ways, his lines, the informal school will be little more than the old system in a new disguise. However, if he is too passive, allowing anarchy and indulgence to prevail, the new school may be rather like some of the least structured progressive schools. Silberman speaks about the "right balance" between allowing the child's interests to guide the educational process and allowing the teacher to guide the child toward the knowledge, skill, and development of self-discipline. However, he gives the reader no set of indicators by which he can discern if such a balance exists in a classroom under observation. Even in these general terms, he leaves the range quite open, stating at one point about the system he approves, ". . . the teachers and administrators with whom I talked and whose informal classrooms I observed were more than simply 'here'; they were very much in charge" (p. 210). Discussing Piaget's contribution to what educational practice ought to be, Silberman says that "the child is the principal agent in his own education and mental development" (p. 215).

Silberman recognizes the pivotal nature of teacher education for the translation of the informal school idea into practice. But several of the measures he suggests are so vague that they amount to a statement of faith or expression of sentiment. For instance, he urges that teachers should think about education, that the teacher should be infused with purpose. Hence, like many others, Silberman is frequently in the re-endorsing the banners stage rather than in the stage of program development (which in itself is only the second step on the long road to societal change).

Particularly naive are Silberman's implicit assumptions about the societal anchoring of the present structure and the conditions under which it may be unlocked and reshaped. The *I.D.E.A. Reporter* ("News from the World of Education"), summarizes Silberman's message on this point: ". . . by and large, teachers, principals, and superintendents are decent, intelligent, and caring people who try to do their best by their lights. If they make a botch of it, and an uncomfortably large number do, it is because it simply never occurs to more than a handful to ask *why* they are doing what they are doing—to think seriously or deeply about the purposes or consequences of education." (3) Silberman's theory is not quite that simple, but almost so.

Silberman endorses the idea that all students should do some teaching as a major way to humanize them and that all university departments should make teacher education one of their prime goals. But, one must ask, is it accidental that these ideas, which are not completely novel, have not been implemented so far? Are there other values which will have to be sacrificed to maximize this educational one? Are there deep-seated interests which are being challenged? These are problems of substantive rationality (multiplicity of purposes) and politics (how sufficient support may be marshalled for the desired change). Without some answer to these kinds of questions, no idea can be realistically specified.

While Silberman generally stays on a level of generality, which in a sense protects the ideas he promotes, at one key juncture his vagueness casts doubt on the validity of the whole conception. This concerns his evidence.

<u>On the Role of Data</u>   Ideas fly cheaply, evidence is hard to muster. Hence, ideas which are substantiated by evidence, supported by data that they "work," are to be particularly treasured. Before turning to the essence of the data on the merits of informal schools, let me say that, throughout the book, the research Silberman and his staff undertook is not of high quality. In their attempts to substantiate a point, they frequently draw on sources even vaguer and more immune to evidence than Silberman himself. For instance, so what if Paul Goodman "argues" that "technology *is* a branch of moral philosophy" (p. 388) or if Harold Taylor has said that "preparing to become a teacher is like preparing to become a poet"?(p. 380) Does this co-endorsement of banners make them wiser, more useful, and indeed more authoritative? Whole books, some of which are edited collections of papers, are cited as sources of evidence for specific points (footnote 7, page 19). And statistical data is used in a rather relaxed manner.

Silberman relies heavily on journalistic observations of the "I-have-seen-it-myself" type. I am among those sociologists who maintain that such data is often as good a source as quantitative data and that is almost invariably a valuable complement to quantitative data. However, one must separate credible from tendentious reporting. When I read that in a primary school in Oxfordshire "there is no ambivalence about authority and no confusion about roles" and that in an infant school in London we find ". . . the combination of great joy and spontaneity and activity with equally great self-control and order" and that "in every formal classroom that I went to visit in England, children were restless" and so on, I take it for granted that such statements are, at least, exaggerated, since very few social phenomena are that monolithic. As Silberman's reporting is loaded with such adjectives, I cannot but start wondering about the reliability of all his first-hand observations.

Second, the well-trained and qualified journalist, anthropologist, and historian has a special sense which allows him to tell the trivial from the consequential. It is a poor journalist who attempts to use the trivial to claim that it stands for the consequential, which he did not observe and hence cannot report from first hand. Too often Silberman reports relatively trivial items, as follows:

A child who has been seated at a table, writing, hurriedly leaves as she hears the call for physical education. "Come back, please, Michelle; your chair isn't put back," the teacher softly calls to her. "We don't have very many rules," the teacher tells the visitor, "but children must learn to look after the property and put things back where they belong." (p. 227)

A school in Leicestershire. In a corner where two main corridors meet, is a large table with a sign in large letters reading, "Smell everything on this table." On the table are a number of jars, of rose petals, of mixed flowers, of vanilla, coffee, cloves, and various other herbs and spices. (p. 224)

Thus, it is not Silberman's journalistic approach to data which weakens his case, but his weak journalism softens the data.

This weakness chiefly concerns secondary points; the main empirical softness is found in the lack of clarity concerning schools which have been successfully informalized. Silberman recommends informal schools on the basis of "it has been done, successfully, in Britain" (and in a few cases in the United States). That is, there *are* viable prototypes. The evidence of success of these schools is, by necessity, limited and incomplete since the approach is fairly new and full evaluation is very difficult. But the very fact that schools can be organized in this way, and that they graduate students who are at least not very poorly educated, is itself of great significance.

One must then ask—*which* schools have been informalized in Britain? Are these infant schools (age 5 to 7) *or* schools in general, including secondary ones? It is a very different proposition to state that the first grade should be quite similar to the kindergarten and to limit the informalization largely to the first two school years, than to state that "schools" should be full of learn-through-play, do-your-own-thing and so on. At one point Silberman makes quite clear that the British experience is much more extensive in infant schools than in higher grades of primary schools. Infant schools provide much of the "it works" data and they are frequently cited as the source of his first-hand observations. However, in contrast to the factual materials presented, his discussion tends to imply that at least all grades of the primary school should be informalized and, to a somewhat lesser extent, also those of the secondary schools. To put it more sharply—where the evidence is relatively solid, for the "infant age,"—the recommendations offer little that is new either for educational thought *or* practice; where the recommendation requires far-reaching changes, it has little grounding in empirical reality.(4)

Furthermore, the data gives an unclear picture as to the value of these schools for pupils from a working class or lower middle class background. It is also unclear whether there are special factors in Britain which are not transferable to American schools; for example, the role of the principal seems to be quite different in the two school systems. Finally, as long as attendance is required, children are evaluated (graded), and many parents demand "achievements," it is unclear if informalized schools will really be fundamentally different from the existing ones—an assumption which runs throughout Silberman's book.

Human Nature, Institutionalization, and Piaget   Any educational theory is predicated on certain implicit or explicit assumptions about human nature. To what extent is man open to instruction or is he biologically pre-determined? And, is man straining toward the light of reason or must he be coaxed to look at it? The prevailing view of man's nature in the social sciences and in the educational establishment downgrades biological factors (often viewed as racist) and tends to assume that man is very educable. Silberman subscribes to this highly optimistic position.

Among the optimists, there are those who see man taking to education as naturally as a duck to water; this propensity approximates the unfolding of an instinct, which can be helped or hindered by the educational institutions, but which cannot be fundamentally shaped by them. Piaget's theory, which Silberman embraces, is interpreted as a major support of this view.

This great confidence in human nature is coupled with a great suspicion of institutions. Schools, at least as they are presently constituted, are viewed as hindering or distorting this natural development. The more extreme proponents favor doing away with schools as institutions. The more moderate counsellors, like Silberman, favor, in effect, curbing their scope, reducing their institutionalization, and restructuring the remaining elements in such a way that the child is helped in his growth rather than being directed. The informalizers stress the second element (of help), while the liberators concentrate on the first (reducing the scope). Silberman's program is rich in both, although he talks as if it is chiefly a matter of moving from control to assistance.

My view of human nature is less optimistic. Recent evidence suggests that physiological factors (such as nourishment) and social background factors (such as those recorded by the Coleman report and studies by compensatory educators) are quite powerful. As a result, we see that pre-school and extra-school forces can damage many children to the point where their "pre-programmed" sequence of capacities, as Piaget followers see them, are so severely disturbed that they will not unfold and can be tapped by the *educator only through very great efforts and costs.* For me, the normative conclusion derived from this evidence is *not* to reduce our educational efforts for the disadvantaged, but to start earlier, to move more broadly, to be more persistent, and to invest many more resources in such efforts. But, it also means that school organization and curriculum often cannot be based on an optimistic assumption about the unfolding natural powers of the child. Educators must recognize that the natural sequence is often derailed and that only large guided efforts *on their side* can put the child back on this high actualization track.

Also, it must be noted that Piaget's work refers to stages of learning in which the *inner capacities* blossom; but, there is no evidence to show that these capacities will be actualized unless actualization is *systematically* encouraged. One cannot derive from man's capacity to walk on two legs the assumption that he will unless he is actively taught to do so. Nor can one assume that a child, possessing a certain natural capacity, also possesses a natural motivation to exercise it.

The critical question becomes then—how much, how detailed, how encompassing a guiding hand is needed? Silberman does not hold the radical position, which in effect eliminates such guidance; he does see a role for a teacher. But, he philosophically leans towards a teacher who is child-centered, not in the sense of responding to the child's underlying capacities, but to his *expressed* needs. Informalization aims to give prime emphasis to the child's *interests,* which may or may not correspond with his natural capacities, and to construct the educational process around his wishes.

In my opinion, the majority of the children in *our* society need more of a guiding hand, a more institutionalized school than the highly informal school that the theorists advocate. A school system is needed which exercises less control than the present but provides more guidance than the one Silberman advocates. The exact mix cannot be spelled out within the limits of a review essay. Nor should it be based on idle speculation; different mixes should be tried and evaluated. It may well be established that children who come from privileged homes, often inconsistent or ultra permissive, may have to learn to function with a *somewhat* more structured environment. No society could function if all its members acted as selfishly as those who seek to maximize their freedoms, disregarding the costs such maximization imposes on others. Children from lower middle-class homes may have to be guided in learning to cope with more freedom than they are accustomed to, so that they will not backlash in frustration when they are given more of it. (Possibly here the first grades would be more formal than the later ones, within the primary school, to reduce the discontinuity in the transition from the authoritarian home to the informal school.) A still different approach may have to be designed for those whose natural potential capacities have been suppressed by the conditions which prevail in disadvantaged communities. The concept of the same school structure for all never had any broad reality in a society where children come from such divergent starting points. Children may now go to what looks like the same school but actually there are great differences among schools in the way the same rules and organizational principles are applied, and these differences are correlated with class background. Nor has the notion of one school for all, on the face of it a great equality, any normative validity. "Informality for all" is no more realistic than assuming you can teach all fifth graders the same math just because the Piaget scheme suggests that they all ought to be "ready" for it.

Most important of all, the school is unavoidably a funnel which leads from infancy at home to the adult occupational structure in the greater society. Hence, just as earlier grades are and ought to be much more like home, the later grades ought to be more like the society in which the students will live. This ought to be a better society than the present one; hence the higher grades may be geared not only to the present, but also to a brighter future, although not to a utopia. Otherwise, one burdens the educational system with more pressures than it can possibly sustain; this in turn could backfire both against the schools and their graduates. Therefore, an adequate theory of education requires a conception of the society from which the child comes and which he will enter as an adult—and an understanding of the amount of leverage the school can be reasonably expected to have on either of these aspects of society. To reiterate, I see the backgrounds of the majority of children as highly suppressive to their natural capacities and hence, the school organization, first of all, must serve a corrective function for these. It is not only the disadvantaged who are in need of decompressive education, but also those from the silent majority and from ultra permissive or inconsistent homes.(5) It is precisely in this area that the school's greatest potential leverage lies, especially if it works in connection with other social institutions, ranging in scope from labor exchanges to housing authorities.

Considerations of the society into which the students will graduate are equally important; it is unfair and unrealistic to prepare them for the educator's favorite dream world because education does not have the force to transform society. Hence, educating students for life in a society which does not exist, say in Silberman's "humane and just society" or for one in which work is as much fun as play—will *not* yield such a society, but might well serve to prepare a frustrated and disillusioned generation of graduates. Moreover, the students mostly are much too smart for such schemes to succeed *in* school, especially in high school and college; they seek education which has a reality and when this is not given —the educator's utopianism becomes a major alienating factor.

Silberman correctly stresses that our schools are organized as if everyone will graduate either to work on an assembly line or in a civil service. They are best suited to preparing indifferent cogs for an industrial-bureaucratic machinery, that is, at best, to be part of yesterday's world. Schools must, hence, be recognized, not just in the substance of their teaching but in the very educational environment and experience they provide, to prepare their students for the different societies of 1980 and even for the year 2000 and beyond. But, despite the hip talk about rapid societal change, as far as I can foresee, our society will continue to have major instrumental and technical needs. True, we will be able to work less, and less efficiently, and still be affluent. And we can realistically help prepare students for a world with more "work" and less "labor" (to use Hannah Arendt's terms) and a world in which more energy and time are devoted to personal and interpersonal growth, and less to productivity—all educational purposes for which informal schooling is suited. However, we must also recognize that the transition from one societal pattern to another will not be abrupt, even if there will be a radical revolution, and a revolution does not seem imminent. Hence, schools must help prepare the child for a better society but unfortunately it is premature to prepare him for the good society. To cease to educate children for discipline or to put a ceiling on their spontaneity, to build up their intolerance for periods of labor, and their acceptance of rules and authority—is to prevent the educational system from helping to bring about that change for which the society is *ripe*. Our efforts to prepare students for a society that may exist at a later time or for a society which cannot exist *reduces* the impact of the educational system, as an agent of societal change. Its graduates will be too utopia-minded to join with other groups working for societal change, and this in turn will lead the graduates to withdraw into apathy, romantic revolutionary infantile acts, or to reject their education in favor of the world around them, as it is. The well-known principle of physical education applies here: one helps the pupil to evolve goals which require that he stretch his muscles, but not to run one mile in three minutes. One helps the pupil to raise his sights, as his actualized capacities (as distinct from his potential ones) grow. Such a posture would spell, for the organization of schools, moving from a relatively informal organization in the early years (subject to great variations according to varying decompressive needs) to a *relatively* less informal, more uniform, more specialized schooling as we move closer to graduation.

It may seem ungrateful to a book which raises many provocative issues to conclude by saying that the best we can hope to do is to outgrow it rapidly—both as a policy guide for educational reforms and as a form of policy research. But this recommendation seems appropriate not only for this work but for many which recently provided a stimulating but also "soft" basis for new policy making in education and societal guidance in general.

Asking the Right Questions

Frank G. Jennings

Society educates its members more profoundly and more last-ingly than family, church, or school. For good and for ill, we are what we become because of where and when we are born. Hunger shapes us. So do the love and hate of our neighbors. Chance enlarges our vision or blinds us to opportunities we would not know how to seize. The only hope of orderly freedom we can reasonably build must be made in classrooms in the few thousand precious days that span our childhood and youth, for society is grossly evenhanded. It takes us where we are at birth and keeps us among our closest, ungiving kind.

Only the school can give us a sense of horizon, can open us up to

Reprinted by permission from *Saturday Review*, Oct. 17, 1970, 66-8. Copyright: 1970 *Saturday Review*, Inc. Mr. Jennings is editor-at-large of *Saturday Review* and associated with New World Foundation.

possibilities, can help us to learn how to discover and use our special talents and private hungers. Only the school can arm us with the wit and the strategies to make society more generous than we think it can be.

But our schools are always failing us, promising us magic and providing a dull routine that leads to emotional and intellectual life at the subsistence level. Our schools are mindless, dull, and drab, whether they are moldering in slums or shining brightly on suburban hillsides. This is the large and shattering half-truth about education in the eighth decade of the American Century.

Thus does Charles E. Silberman in his new book *Crisis in the Classroom* try to spell out the familiar indictment of our schools. He succeeds with greater precision and more dispassionate documentation than any critic of the past three decades. Nothing that he has to say in this matter should surprise or shock anyone who has worried about this state of affairs. But Silberman has thought long and hard and purposively about education's estate, and the result is a book different from and more useful than anything that has gone before his work.

For Silberman is concerned with the tension between the powerful societal forces that "educate" in the larger sense: the mass media, the social institutions, the very culture that surrounds us, and the schools wherein we attempt to create newer and more effective kinds of sense and order within ourselves and so, eventually, within the society that we live in.

That tension is necessary, for without it we are doomed to live as ants or bees; but it is dangerous, for there is no assurance of any external beneficent "control" that will make things turn out right, that will assure equality of educational opportunity, that will guarantee intellectual and emotional outcomes that are humane and liberating for the individual and his group.

"The test of society," says Silberman, "as of an institution, is not whether it is improving, although certainly such a test is relevant, but whether it is adequate to the needs of the present and of the foreseeable future. Our educating institutions fail that test: schools, colleges, churches, newspapers, magazines, television stations and networks, all fall short of what they could be, of what they *must* be if we are to find meaning and purpose in our lives, in our society, and in our world."

This book had its genesis some four years ago, when the Carnegie Corporation invited Silberman to undertake a study of teacher education. But it soon became obvious that one cannot merely examine the education and the making of teachers. It is necessary, in our complex, ever changing society, to try to understand the way the whole culture informs and educates each citizen.

The Greeks called this process the *paideia*. Thus, all the professions, the businesses, the industries, the political, social, and fraternal organizations, the pervasive mass media, the passing fads and public angers—all of these *educate* us. As Silberman realized early in his study:

The contemporary American is educated by his *paideia* no less than the Athenian was by his. The weakness of American education is not that the *paideia* does not educate, but that it educates to the wrong ends.

Both Alfred North Whitehead and John Dewey are the modern world's pre-eminent guides to appropriate means and ends in education, and Silberman makes exquisite use of their wisdom. Thus he insists that:

. . . education is defined . . . as the deliberate or purposeful creation, evocation, or transmission of knowledge, abilities, skills, and values. To emphasize the deliberate and the purposeful is not to deny that nondeliberate influences may be more powerful; it is to assert that man cannot depend upon a casual process of learning. Unless men are forced to rediscover all knowledge for themselves (which is patently impossible), they must be educated, which is to say that education, to be education, must be purposeful.

And there's the rub. Our American schooling systems are not purposeful. One of our egalitarian glories is that much of their origins have been ad hoc. They are task-oriented and job-specific. We make better engineers, farmers, physicians, ministers of our competing faiths, scientists, and restaurateurs. We want their services. We are rarely, if ever, concerned about the quality of their minds. We are distrustful of men with missions. We are uncomfortable before a display of fervor. We want our "rights," but we do not want them to be programmed for us. And yet we are haunted by the disorder of our values, by the discontinuities between our beliefs and our behaviors.

Silberman argues for a transformation of the schools and of teaching, which, to the degree that it is successful, will produce those salutary changes that might assure survival of the world as we know it can be. Silberman has found, especially in the infant-school movement in England, and in its adaptations in this country, strong evidence that the best of American progressive education is still vital and profoundly relevant to our contemporary needs. He has stopped at islands of sanity in slum schools and in rural colleges. He has seen splendid teachers being produced in the New School of Behavioral Studies in Education in North Dakota. He has found high schools of great promise in Philadelphia's Parkway Program and in the John Adams High School in Portland, Oregon. He has witnessed teachers, ordinary, not especially gifted teachers, re-creating themselves as more open, alert, and caring people, able to match new skill to keener insight, and marshal both in the service of their students. He has talked with principals, deans, and other administrators, some reluctant, some fearful, but many who are willing to chance, not another "innovation," but a basic reordering of their commitments and their tasks.

Despite the aching fact that we as a nation are in deep and anguished trouble, from the White House to our cities' wastelands, which Silberman assesses with firm compassion, he has the courage to insist that our society *is* improving. By any measure, and at any level, our schools are performing better than they have in the past.

The United States has succeeded in doing what, until very recently, almost every European educator and a good many Americans insisted could *not* be done. It has managed to insure intellectual excellence and creative scholarship in a system of higher education. It has combined what the sociologist Martin Trow calls the traditional or "elite" function of the university—the transmission of high culture and the creation of new knowledge—with its "popular" functions, i.e., educating large numbers of students, particularly for the professions and vocations, and providing other services to the society.

This is not to suggest that Silberman is either more genteel or more naively sanguine than the romantic critics of the most recent past. His indictments are more precise than Edgar Z. Freidenberg's, more maturely informed than Jonathan Kozol's, more responsibly programmatic than John Holt's. His philosophical analyses are more logically (and psychologically) consistent than Paul Goodman's. Silberman has been paying his dues of attention in the real coin of social commitment for a long time, and he does his civics homework.

The crises in education, like all our other disruptions and discontinuities, cannot be abated, cannot be weathered, by mere patchwork strategies, nor do we have the luxury of stopping the world and time until we can devise and re-create it closer to some heart's desire. Society must be re-created out of and within what it is and what it has.

Crisis in the Classroom attempts, gloriously, to show how this task may be accomplished. Yet, I feel protective of this book, perhaps because I have watched it grow from an idea to a proposal, to a blue-covered first draft, to several salmon-covered "rewrites," and on to a ten-pound manuscript that was transmuted into galleys, some of which were being recast, to include newer awarenesses, even as the book was being readied for its first pressrun.

That book is in hand now, and it is short of perfection, which is a way of saying that it is a work of art. To be merely accurate is to record some simple aspect of reality and to tell the lie that it is easily remedied. To be unequivocal is to come to certainty about small and safe matters and to suggest that they embody our universals. Silberman equivocates. He takes hunches and rides them far, for he chances the artist's risk. He will disturb many readers, especially some of the professionals, for he has points of view. He is selective. He has preferences. He is passionate, less in what he condemns than in what he espouses. He is insistent in the questions he asks. He has gone, an earnest scholar, to the great sources. He has read, and he has understood much, and he is not afraid of being confused. If only some of the more ardent educators and their critics would undergo the pains of learning that Silberman has accepted, how much clearer would their visions be, how much better would their plans survive the tests of action.

Initially, as has been noted earlier, this had been proposed as a study of the "education of educators." Silberman had planned to learn how all, who in any significant way affect what goes on in the schools and in the minds of citizens, are themselves educated. He wanted to understand what their world views are, how they come by their images of man, what their concept of the good life is, and how they act upon the premises hidden within such notions.

In that undertaking, Silberman's success is modestly incomplete. He has a good sense of the ferment in medical and legal education, some sure understanding of what is happening in schools of engineering. He has a fuller comprehension of curricular conditions in liberal arts undergraduate education. In the latter institutions, his judgments, while not new in any crucial way, are healthily harsh. For the liberal arts college is still the keystone experience for all higher education and almost all professional education. Most of our classroom teachers come out of four-year undergraduate liberal arts colleges. Most of those schools have been very little moved by the various curricular revolutions that have whirled through education in the past half-century. Because of this, our universities do not possess much *universitas*. They are semiprivate holdings within the commonwealth. They are separated from all of their communities and publics. They pay modified homage to society; they offer conditional allegiance to the public; they are sources of convertible wealth for the nation, but at best they are "cousins germane" to the polity.

Our present troubles began, Silberman insists, at the turn of the century when education went public in a big way and turned professional. Educators were divorced from the liberal arts faculties who tended to regard concerns of schooling and learning as beneath their dignity, fit subjects only for the second-class citizens of academe, the educationists. Thus, "many departments of history, philosophy, sociology, and psychology, including some of the most distinguished, quite literally do not have a single member with any interest in the problems of the schools."

If *Crisis in the Classroom* has a central purpose, it is to set aside that bill of divorcement, to bring the estranged members together in a family again. For there is more at stake than pride and status, there is more to be gained than an orderly household. The lives of all our children and the very mindedness of society itself cannot be made whole as long as educators are obsessed by indecent needs to defend their own turfs, and academics regard those turfs as stinking kitchen middens.

It is a peculiarly American presumption that one can take a major work and assess it in a few acerbic paragraphs, subjecting it to a putative test of relevance by semiprofessional scholarship, largely gleaned from the work itself, and either dismiss the effort or announce the "achievement" without ever meeting the intellectual challenge of its author. Charles E. Silberman deserves the psychic income of being used for the ends he has pursued.

None of what he says is new. What is new is that one man has submitted himself to the task of trying to learn what information the new maps of education contain, and what is still of great value in the old charts. He has read and understood John Dewey (would that more educationists could read as well as Silberman does). He has read Comenius and Pestalozzi. He has comprehended Whitehead, Erikson, Bruner, and Piaget. He has been informed by Paul Goodman, Kenneth Kenniston, Noam Chomsky, and Robert Merton. He has gone to the slums and ghettos and discovered vital seeds of hope among the barren rubble of crushed ideals. He has been profoundly influenced by Lawrence A. Cremin in framing and asking hard questions about purpose. He has learned that the school can and must be "a center of inquiry" in which all teachers are always students of teaching, in which our children and youth are never merely objects. For, as Silberman concludes this brave and powerful social inquiry:

. . . when schools become warm and humane, teachers grow as human beings as well as teachers. The lesson is clear; Dewey stated it two-thirds of a century ago. What is needed, he wrote, "is improvement of education, not merely by turning out teachers who can do better the things that are necessary to do, but rather changing the conception of what constitutes education."

So educators should be told: Read *Crisis in the Classroom*. Do not contend with it. Do not tell Silberman that he should have written your book. Take your charts, which he has scanned with admiration and anguish, and rebuild the schools as only you are able to.

Legislators and their attendant bureaucrats must be told: Accept the study as the most generous and hopeful expression of the yet-to-be-realized American genius for education, and match it with a more mindful *paideia* than we now possess. Begin at last a lifetime of making this nation mirror its sacred trust. Much more than money is required. Politics must rejoin public purpose. It is once again social seedtime.

Foundation executives and their staffs must be told: Be more mindful in your civic generosity than you have been in the recent past. You hold in trust the most valuable of all venture capital. Use it more sparingly, spread it more widely, be more precise in your giving, more courageous in the face of its consequences. Use *Crisis in the Classroom* as a handbook in social enterprise.

Finally, the citizen-reader must be told: This book is commended to you most prayerfully. It is not a weapon to be used to terrorize the school board or the university. It is a thesaurus of creative questions which, by asking, you may help the schools in our Promethean task. As we teach one another, so will we liberate the teachers of our children to treasure the unique worth of every man, to diminish the value of no man, and to liberate the genius for life that is in all of us.

Review of *Crisis in the Classroom*

John H. Fischer

Charles E. Silberman's report on the present state of American schools has been hailed by many and will be praised by more, but some will accuse him of excessive kindness to the educational establishment. There will be, too, the insecure professionals, always ready to eject the uncredentialed poacher from the preserve. And there will be those who will see that Silberman has had the courage to attack an enormously complex task and the competence and character to perform it with thoroughness, balance, insight, and compassion. The result is neither another prescription of sentimental panaceas nor one more cheap exercise in polemic propaganda. This is a searching effort to define what ails our schools and to propose alternatives for improving them that are at once sound, hopeful, and workable.

Anyone sufficiently familiar with American public schools to

Reprinted by permission from *The Phi Delta Kappan*, Jan. 1971, 313-14.
Mr. Fischer is President of Teachers College, Columbia University.

write about them with respectable authority knows that any appraisal, from the most negative criticism to the most extravagant praise, can be justified by examples drawn from life. Because Charles Silberman knows not only this range of quality and character but also where the balance falls, he is aware of how grievously and how often the weaknesses of our schools diminish the lives of our children.

He seeks no villains and he finds none. "By and large," he says, "teachers, principals, and superintendents are decent, intelligent, caring people who try to do their best by their lights." But good intentions conceded, "adults take the schools so much for granted they fail to appreciate what joyless places most American schools are, how oppressive and petty are the rules by which they are governed, how intellectually sterile and aesthetically barren the atmosphere, what an appalling lack of civility obtains on the part of teachers and principals, what contempt they unconsciously display for children as children."

The indictment is harsh—harsh enough to stimulate the predictable and defensive response it has already elicited from some school people. More often than not, however, the attempted refutation only adds substance to the charge. For the typical rejoinder takes the form either that Silberman's appraisal is not valid for a particular school or that he "doesn't understand." Silberman himself insists that there are bright spots among schools, and many of them he recognizes and applauds. He cites them with enthusiastic appreciation by the dozens among the 200 anecdotal "items" he inserts to document the faults he finds and to illustrate the possibilities he describes. Regarding the quality and depth of Silberman's understanding—and sympathy—the book itself, if read, will serve as evidence.

The root of the problem—and the essence of the premise that it can be solved—is that "what is mostly wrong with the public schools is due not to venality or indifference or stupidity but to mindlessness." That mindlessness Silberman sees revealed among professionals and laymen alike in "the failure or refusal to think seriously about educational purpose, the reluctance to question established practice." His criticism gains validity and force because of the breadth of background from which he approaches the question of educational purpose. That Charles Silberman has done his homework will surprise no one who knows his earlier work on the American economic system and his perceptive study of racial integration, *Crisis in Black and White*. From Comenius to Coleman, from Plato to Dewey to Piaget, Silberman has cast a wide net for evidence, argument, and wisdom to illuminate the durable values of education and its present perplexities. His sophisticated acquaintance with educational thought across the centuries, across the country, and across the seas gives him the basis from which to view more than the failures of the schools themselves. He examines also many of the widely publicized proposals put forward in the last two decades by distinguished academicians who finally deigned to take a hand in educational reform and by the technological wizards who were about to mass-produce wisdom. Many of these men, distinguished scholars though they were in other fields, regrettably missed the first step. They disdained any study of the history of education or its reform and so, neglecting Santayana's warning, suffered the fate he predicted for those who ignore the minutes of society's earlier meetings. Because Silberman has avoided the traps into which they fell, his analyses run deep and his proposals respect reality.

If schools are to emerge from the slough of mindless routine in which so many are now mired, Silberman argues that we must first recognize the plight of the teacher. Repeatedly he expresses his conviction that most teachers are honest, willing people doing their best under trying circumstances. Little improvement can be expected unless those circumstances can be altered so as to assure teachers an atmosphere of freedom and trust. As Silberman confidently observes, "If treated as professionals and as people of worth, teachers behave like the caring, concerned people they would like to be." He rejects out of hand the arrogant notion, popularized in the mid-Sixites, of a teacher-proof curriculum.

To illustrate the validity of his confidence in teachers, Silberman draws examples from what many would call the least likely source —the New York City public schools—specifically, schools in Harlem and a heavily Spanish-speaking part of Manhattan's upper West Side. While there are no quick or easy explanations to distinguish these schools from sadly more typical urban institutions, the details of their difference fall under three major headings: humane concern for children as people, positive expectations (of children and teachers), and competent professional leadership.

Item: seated in a big leather club chair, his back to the open door, Seymour Gang (principal of P.S. 192 in Manhattan) is talking to a visitor. A Black sixth grade boy walks in, tiptoes over to Dr. Gang's chair and kisses him on the top of his bald pate, saying, "I'm going to miss you next year, Dr. Gang."

But Seymour Gang's school, like Mrs. Martha Froelich's Finley School in Harlem, stands for more than reciprocated affection between students and staff. In both of their schools, reading has been so effectively taught that in a community plagued by disgracefully low reading scores, their pupils, despite all the familiar problems, approach or exceed national norms. These principals, as Silberman tells us, "not only expect their students to succeed, they hold themselves and their teachers accountable if their students fail."

Three and one-half years of research, much of it spent visiting classrooms and recording at first hand what goes on in them, could hardly be expected to produce complacency about American education. Charles Silberman is far from complacent. But he is confident that schools in all sorts of settings can be made good for children, precisely because he and his staff have seen so many that are. Some of the best of them he has found among English primary schools. For some readers, the most valuable pages of his report will be the descriptions of infant schools in English cities and towns, and of the ways these schools employ flexibility in classroom organization and curriculum design.

Silberman does not agree with those who believe that to answer American problems we have only to import British informality. For one thing, he warns, there is no such thing as *the* informal approach but only a wide variety of specific practices by which teaching and learning can be made consistent with the nature of childhood. Nor is the school's setting in society to be disregarded: "The institutional differences in the ways schools are organized, administered, and financed, along with the cultural differences, especially in the role of the family and of adult authority in general, make it dangerous to try to transfer forms unchanged from one country to another."

One fundamental difference between British and American schools is the generally smaller size of the former, which rarely enroll more than 300 students in a primary unit. Another is the greater autonomy of the British headmaster as compared with the typical American principal. Through the entire volume runs the clear implication that while teachers, superintendents, school boards, parents, and public leaders of all sorts must be involved in the process of reforming American education, the most influential single individual in the entire enterprise may well be the school principal. As this volume so clearly demonstrates, good schools come in many varieties, but neither Silberman nor any other investigator of record has ever suggested that there exists anywhere a superior school without an exceptional head.

Atmosphere, leadership, and organization aside, there remains the crucial matter of professional education. If any fault is to be found with this splendid volume it is that it raises more questions than it answers about the education of teachers and other professionals. That disappointment is sharpened by the difference between the book as it has finally appeared and the initial intent of the project of which it is the result. In 1966 the Carnegie Corporation established its Commission on the Education of Educators and persuaded Mr. Silberman to undertake, with access to the commission's advice (but not dependent on its consent), a study of the role of the university in educating not only teachers and other standard types of "professional educators," but also those who work in the other powerfully educative agencies of society. These, it was soon agreed, would include professionals in the mass media, museums, churches, health agencies, the law, and more.

But Silberman decided that, despite the undeniable power of other forces, schools are the central and basic institution established to promote systematic learning. Hence he concentrated his attention upon schools, although by no means overlooking the other agencies. Indeed, his analysis of their roles, shortcomings, and possibilities, despite its brevity, is perceptive and provocative.

Nor would it be accurate to say he has ignored teacher education. On the contrary, his delineation of the issues, his thoughtful views of the interrelation of the liberal and professional components, and his references to a few of the imaginative new programs, such as the University of North Dakota's New School for Behavioral Studies in Education, not only are valuable substantive contributions, but embody conceptions that invite, and almost surely will have, further development.

It is, of course, impossible to differ with Silberman's assertion that before the issues of teacher education can even be defined, much less resolved, the prior step must be to clarify our expectations of schools, and, most particularly, to specify the purposes schools ought to serve. It is to that first task that this volume is mainly devoted, and it has been accomplished with rationality and persuasiveness. Silberman insists, moreover, that what should be done can be done, and on the irrefutable ground that it is already being done, albeit in too few places, and for too few children.

What we must have now is an equally well-informed and helpful volume on the question that still awaits answering: How are educators—the whole confounded tribe of them, old and new, to be prepared for their frighteningly powerful work? And when that study does appear, one ITEM it might profitably include is a report on the process that produced one rather exceptional educator named Charles Silberman.

The Crisis of Mindlessness

Maxine Greene

This is a time of fundamental uncertainty about the future of American society. Richard Hofstadter speaks of "a crisis of the

Reprinted by permission from *The Record*, vol. 72, no. 1, Sept. 1970, 133041, Teachers College, Columbia University. Dr. Greene is associated with Teachers College of Columbia University.

spirit"; Arthur M. Schlesinger, Jr., of "an extreme crisis of confidence." The pervasive malaise, the sense of unease have inevitably affected thinking about the public schools. There are those who would like to see the schools return to the teaching of traditional pieties and become bulwarks against "anarchy," perhaps even against change. There are others who perceive the schools as agents of a manipulative "establishment" and assert that only a system of independent schools can liberate the young to learn for themselves. It has long been assumed that education is somehow related to social change; but, in recent years, there has been little talk about *how* the schools bring change about or what that change ought to be. In 1937, John Dewey wrote that "the problem is not whether the schools *should* participate in the production of a future society (since they do anyway) but whether they should do it blindly and irresponsibly, or with the maximum possible of courageous intelligence and responsibility." Now Charles E. Silberman is saying that "mindlessness" accounts for what is wrong with American education. He means "the failure or refusal to think seriously about educational purpose, the reluctance to question established practice"—the very blindness and irresponsibility which concerned John Dewey thirty-three years ago.

Crisis in the Classroom was originally commissioned by the Carnegie Corporation of New York as part of the Carnegie Study of the Education of Educators. In the skilled, professional hands of Charles Silberman (working with an obviously gifted research staff), the book has become a fairly definitive overview of the state of American education today. Following Dewey and Lawrence A. Cremin, he recognizes that 'education' is a more inclusive concept than 'schooling' and devotes considerable space to universities, mass media, libraries, social agencies, the armed forces, and other institutions which educate with varying degrees of deliberateness. His main focus, however, is on the public school; and his primary objective, as we understand it, is to overcome mindlessness by indicating what can be done within the public school by individuals willing to think about what they are doing. If mindlessness is corrected by the kind of thinking which puts the child and his requirements above the demands of scheduling and order, he says, it will become possible to begin educating "for a creative, humane, sensitive life." Education consciously directed to such an end will lead to the emergence of a humane society, or what Dewey used to call a "learning society." The interesting thing about Silberman is that he appears to be convinced this *can* happen and *will* happen, cultural crises despite. His book, therefore, is tonic and heuristic. Identifying specific possibilities of change and renewal, presenting a variety of models, it is clearly intended to stimulate people now working in the public schools to initiate their own reforms.

Silberman is a member of the board of editors of *Fortune* magazine and the author of two widely read books: *The Myths of Automation* and *Crisis in Black and White*. He has taught at Columbia University and City College; but he is neither an academic nor an educationist. His vantage point is that of the informed, interested journalist recently introduced to a challenging new field by such prominent insiders as John Goodlad, Lawrence Cremin, and Kenneth Clark. During the three and a half years in which his book has been in preparation, he and his staff have traveled much, in this country and in England; and they have observed expertly, often with empathy.

There are, in consequence, numerous "items," anecdotal reports of what actually happens in classrooms: dreadful incidents of maltreatment and humiliation; examples of "informal education" at its best; instances of discovery and cognitive learning which are a delight to read. Some of the concreteness and immediacy of Philip W. Jackson's *Life In Classrooms* (an important resource for Silberman) is present in these pages; and there are moments when particular children come to life and steal the scene. Gazella, observed in a Harlem school, is one. She "has been flirting as she works with pencil and paper" and hands the visitor a note saying that she has a new teacher, and "I feel good and not bad." Denise is another: she promises to teach the visitor a new game "another day." Mexican children create a "talking mural" about a citrus grove; one of Arthur Pearl's black freshmen at the University of Oregon tells how "Pearl builds something in you—strength"; self-confident British primary school children weigh and measure in preparation for baking a cake; a little boy in North Dakota, working with a complicated mathematical game, tells the visitor, "Last year we had to work all the time. Now we can play all the time." Somehow, especially in the informal classroom, the sound of vitality is made audible; learning is made visible—interested children learning how to learn.

Spontaneity, activity, joy: these are the great goods for Charles Silberman; and he is convinced they are realizable in every public school. He is capable of the same outrage and indignation the various "romantic" critics express when confronted with sterility in the classroom, tasteless atmospheres, the obsession with order and control. In fact, when selections from his book were published in *The Atlantic Monthly,* they were entitled "Murder in the Schoolroom." But, for all his shocked anger in the face of what Erik Erikson calls the "mutilation" of children's minds, Silberman differentiates himself sharply from critics of education like Edgar Friedenberg, John Holt, Jonathan Kozol, and (to some degree) Paul Goodman. Reading them, he writes, "one might think that the schools are staffed by sadists and clods who are drawn into teaching by the lure of upward mobility and the opportunity to take out their anger . . . on their students." He goes on:

This impression is conveyed less by explicit statement than by nuance and tone—a kind of "aristocratic insouciance," as David Riesman calls it, which these writers affect, in turn reflecting the general snobbery of the educated upper middle class toward the white collar, lower middle-class world of teachers, social workers, and policemen. This snobbery has become, in recent years, a nasty and sometimes spiteful form of big-otry on the part of many selfmade intellectuals, who seem to feel the need to demonstrate their moral and cultural superiority to the lower middle class from which they escaped.

Silberman makes the significant point that most teachers are "decent, honest, well-intentioned" people who behave like "the caring, concerned people they would like to be" once they find themselves in an "atmosphere of freedom and trust." Referring to *The School As A Center of Inquiry* (by Teachers College's Dean Robert Schaefer), he reminds the reader of the dreariness, the loneliness, the "blight" characteristic of most teachers' physical and social environments. If set free to open their own classrooms for talk, activity, and engaged learning, teachers might well give up their preoccupation with rules and regulations. All depends on how they are evaluated and on what help is provided. Silberman finds much to admire in the administrative flexibility achieved by Brit-ish schools and in the functions of the teaching "Head" of each new primary school. Administrators, supervisors, *and* teachers, he suggests, should collaborate in maximizing occasions for learning and structuring environments which change in response to children's interests and activities. But the teacher should be granted a meaningful autonomy, so that he or she also can be liberated to inquire and (in responding to diverse children) to learn.

It is evident that the thought of John Dewey, or some aspects of his thought, has had a pronounced effect on Silberman; and, unlike certain curriculum reformers of the past decade, he openly ac-knowledges his debt. This is not to say, however, that *Crisis in the Classroom* is a latter-day argument for "progressive education" as it developed in the '20s and '30s. Silberman speaks several times of the "vulgarization" of Dewey's ideas, of progressive schools which were "perversions of the ideal." He uses Dewey's argument in *Ex-perience And Education* and in a *New Republic* article written in 1930 to emphasize Dewey's own skepticism with respect to progressivism as it developed over time. ("The weakness of ex-isting progressive education," wrote Dewey, "is due to the meager knowledge which anyone has regarding the conditions and laws of continuity which govern the development of mental power.") The main point, of course, was—as Dewey also said—that too many progressive schools lacked "intellectual control through significant subject matter"; and this is part of what contributed to the demise of progressivism after the 1930s. But Silberman lays considerable stress upon the "success" of progressivism in this country in those early days and lists a number of school systems which instituted progressive programs or "aspects of progressive techniques." We find a degree of over-simplification in this, as we do in Silberman's assertion that "The experience of history thus suggests that Americans, no less than Englishmen, are capable of accepting informal education for their children."

The opening chapters of the book, do, however, succeed in defining present situations in which Dewey's relevance is being newly recognized. As a matter of fact, we can think of few current texts which provide such an inclusive and readable overview of recent educational history. Silberman pays proper heed to unrest, disruption, and changing expectations; to the predicaments of higher education; to the troublesome confusion of "authority" with "power"; to the changes in life-style to which the media (mindlessly) respond. He retraces the immigrant experiences, the development of the "meritocracy," the rise of a "credential" society, the problems of poverty, and the difficulties facing the urban schools.

Not only does he make the issue of disadvantage central; he presents a detailed and enlightening account of the controversies over the Coleman Report on Educational Equality and, most particularly, over the notorious article written by Arthur Jensen for the *Harvard Educational Review*. Silberman is to be commended for the clear explication he provides for research that has been over popularized and widely misunderstood. He is to be commended too for his exposure of its loopholes and glaring errors. Without hedging, he says categorically that "Jensen's argument that black-white IQ differences are largely genetic in origin simply does not stand." Jensen's treatment of environment, he adds, is "simplistic almost to the point of caricature"; and he appends a useful discussion (one of the most readable we have seen) of the complex of cultural factors, not necessarily associated with poverty and social class, which inhibit poor children's development. Among these, of course, are the language used, the child-rearing practices, and the values and attitudes transmitted, "all of which may vary substantially from one ethnic, racial, or religious group to another within the same socioeconomic class." Covering Martin Deutsch's research, Basil Bernstein's, and others', Silberman concludes that the failures of the slum schools are mainly due to the peculiar mindlessness which leads people to focus on why disadvantaged children fail instead of turning their attention to the insufficiences of their schools. Summoning the examples of the drop-out street academies and Harlem Prep in New York, talking about the very real achievements of Harlem's John H. Finley School, he shows that when schools are adjusted to fit children, learning (even advances in reading) can begin. When attention is paid to the dangers of self-fulfilling prophecies, when teachers become aware enough to avoid communicating the idea that poor children are "worthless," when something meaningful is done to build self-esteem, disadvantaged children—like all others—begin to respond positively to what is offered in the way of possibility.

None of this is new to readers of journals like *The Record* or *Saturday Review*. None of it will come as a surprise to readers of Herbert Kohl, George Dennison, Paul Goodman, or Kenneth Clark. But there is something encouraging about the fact that a reporter with the "clout" of the Carnegie Corporation behind him feels justified in breaking through the endless debates, the prolonged *mea culpas,* and coming up with positive assertions about a humane education for all. Once again, it comes down to planning for the "open classroom," a richly structured environment, self-motivated activity, and the kind of teaching that is geared to the individual rather than to an undifferentiated "grade."

What of the great educational reforms undertaken before and after the Sputnik panic of 1957? What of all the promises made on behalf of computers and programed instruction? What of the curriculum reform movement and the "teacher-proof curricula" prepared by university men for the schools they had so long ignored? There is a certain irony in the tale, as Silberman tells it; and he tells it sketchily but well. We read again about team teaching, nongraded elementary schools, the "new biology," the "new physics," all repeatedly "blunted," Silberman says, "on the classroom door."

There is a great deal of chatter, to be sure, about teaching students the structure of each discipline, about teaching them how to learn, about teaching basic concepts. . . . But if one looks at what actually goes on in the classroom—the kinds of texts students read and the kind of homework they are assigned as well as the nature of classroom discussion and the kinds of tests teachers give—he discovers that the great bulk of students' time is still devoted to detail, most of it trivial, much of it factually incorrect, and almost all of it unrelated to any concept, structure, cognitive strategy, or indeed anything other than the lesson plan.

The reasons for the failure are manifold. For one thing, the reformers were unaware that almost everything they were saying had been said before by John Dewey, Boyd Bode, Harold Rugg, and others, and that almost everything they were doing had been attempted before. For another thing, "they perpetuated the false dichotomy that the schools must be either child-centered or subject-centered"; and they, in opposition to the "vulgarizers" of progressivism, placed all their emphasis on subject matter and neglected children's needs. Just as important: the reformers did not engage classroom teachers in the development of the new curricula, nor did they encourage (or even permit) a spirit of inquiry among the teachers actually concerned. Moreover, they neglected to ask what Silberman believes to be the crucial questions respecting the purposes of education: questions about the kind of human being they expected to see emerge; questions about the worth of various kinds of knowledge; questions about the direction of social change. Returning to Professor Cremin once again. Silberman underlines the observation that "to refuse to look at curricula in their entirety is to relegate to interschool politics a series of decisions that ought to call into play the most fundamental philosophical principles."

Granting the necessity to "do" philosophy with respect to curriculum and methods of teaching, not to speak of the aims of education, we wonder why Silberman has excluded contemporary educational philosophy from his bibliography. Apart from John Dewey, Alfred North Whitehead and Marjorie Grene are the only practicing twentieth century philosophers he refers to in his text. A man so well-informed about the educational scene cannot be wholly innocent of the work done by men like Philip Phenix, Harry Broudy, James R. McClellan, Jr., I. B. Berkson, B. Othanel Smith, Robert Ennis, Philip Smith, and numerous other scholars in the field. He does justice to the work of Jean Piaget, Noam Chomsky, Robert Merton, Robert Nisbet, Lee Cronbach, and other representatives of the behavioral and social sciences. He properly acknowledges the contributions made to "informal education" by such innovative, creative teachers as Lillian Weber, Lore Rasmussen, and Marie Hughes, each of whom (in New York City, Philadelphia, and Tucson respectively) is providing living proof that the "open classroom" is as feasible in slums as it is in suburbs —in black, white, and Mexican-American communities equally. He recognizes the considerable achievement of the New School of Behavioral Studies in Education in North Dakota; the work done in secondary education by John Bremer in Philadelphia's Parkway Program, and the successful experiment being carried on by Robert Schwartz and his Harvard colleagues at John Adams High School in Oregon.

It is at least worthy of note that, for all his concern with problems distinctively susceptible to philosophical examination, Silberman acknowledges none of the work now being done in language philosophy, moral philosophy, social philosophy, aesthetics, existentialism, or phenomenology. "Philosophy," Dewey wrote in *Democracy And Education,* "is thinking what the known demands of us—what responsive attitude it exacts. It is an idea of what is possible, not an accomplished fact." There is a sense in which Charles Silberman enters the philosophic domain as soon as he begins talking of "what the known demands" and, certainly, when he begins stressing the importance of clear "purposes." His book would have benefited from an exposure to ongoing educational philosophy; the teachers who will read him would be far more likely to think about what they are doing if they could be introduced to the special sort of self-consciousness and clarity made possible by engagement with philosophy.

We feel the lack of a philosophic orientation most keenly when we reach the proposals for teacher education with which this fine, flawed book concludes. Whitehead provides the text at this point: only teachers who are free can work to liberate the young. Silberman, still depending on John Dewey and his notion of continuing learning, says eloquently: "To be an educator is to understand something of how to make one's education effective in the real world, of how to apply knowledge to the life one lives and the society in which one lives it—in a word, to know what is relevant —and how to make knowledge relevant." Teaching, he dares to say, is "the ultimate liberal art"; and educating teachers should be a central concern of the college or university. The rich, spontaneous educational experiences described in the course of the book can only be assured when there is a "synergistic relationship between the colleges and universities and the public schools," when the serious study of education and educational purpose becomes the core of the liberal arts curriculum.

Quixotic? Perhaps. Utopian? Maybe so. Nevertheless, we think Charles Silberman has performed a great service, if only because his book may stimulate individuals to effect some changes in their own classrooms. At this moment in our history, that may be enough to expect. The increasing polarization of our nation; the continuing war; the "benign neglect"—not only of black people's needs, but of educational needs—being practiced by the federal government; the threats of repression: all these factors prevent us from sharing Silberman's appealing optimism.

We share his hopes for a humane society. We are pleased and impressed by his Deweyan affirmations. We also believe that free days, open classrooms, and carefully structured learning environments will save the lives of many schoolchildren and help them learn to learn. But we are much afraid that the "mindlessness" so effectively challenged by Charles Silberman is not the only obstacle to a transformation of the schools. There may be an entire civilization to be remade.

Notes

1. I prefer the term *societal guidance* over that of *social engineering*. I use the archaic term "societal" to stress that we are dealing with change in societies and not with changes of a few social relations. The processes involved in societal guidance cannot be ordered or streamlined as is implied by the concept of *engineering* nor can solutions be found on the basis of expert or elite decisions, which the concept of engineering implies.

   Social systems do change constantly as a result of forces which the members do not understand nor control. The concept of guidance points to those changes which society brings about deliberately. For additional discussion see my *The Active Society* (New York: The Free Press, 1968).
2. For the most recent document see *Toward Balanced Growth: Quantity with Quality*. Report of the National Goals Research Staff (Washington, D. C.: Government Printing Office, 1970).
3. (Summer, 1970) p.1.
4. To cite a journalistic source, William K. Stevens' report *(New York Times,* October 19, 1970, p.29) about "Oregon High School's Experiment in Free Study" that

   A survey of students indicated that they considered Adams a "humanized" school. "At least you feel like a person here," said one student. But the same survey found that many students felt the intellectual content of the curriculum should be strengthened.

   For discussion of the informal school as being more effective as a source of joy than of achievements, in the traditional sense, see Silberman, pp. 231-32.
5. It may be suggested, at this point, that we fall short by the same criteria we apply to Silberman, of not spelling out and documenting our propositions. It seems, though, proper in a review to cue and indicate, while a $300,000 study report, which stakes claims for policy guidance, may have to go beyond the specificity and empirical validity provided by a review essay.